THE
RUNNER
WHO NEVER
RAN

a Game Warden's Daughter

THE WORKBOOK
REFLECTIONS EDITION

by Karen Swasey

Edited by Lil Barcaski

Published by: GWN Publishing
www.GWNPublishing.com

Cover Design: Kristina Conatser

ISBN: 978-1-959608-37-0

I'd like to dedicate this book to the memory of my parents, John and Jean Swasey.

To all my family and friends who have supported me on all my trails in life.

And to that little small voice, that always whispers in my ear, my angels, who have always been my guiding light.

TABLE OF CONTENTS

THE "RUNNER WHO NEVER RAN"

A Game Warden's Daughter

Since I was a child, I have often been told, you should share your stories and write a book someday. So, here I am making this my first attempt at sharing my journey through the last 60 years of life.

Preface... It all started in a small western town amongst the mountains of Maine. I have found that if we pay attention to the gifts we receive along the way, that we learn that we are unknowingly equipped to navigate our way through this journey called life. These stories are a reflection of the journey that have become treasures in my life.

When I was a little girl, I remember lying on the grass looking up to the sky knowing that there were angels walking by. My mother would always tell me so. I would stop, look, and say, "But mom, I can't see them." And she would reply, "You need to quiet your soul, be still, be present, and experience the gift of the spirit." So, I would lie there and dream of all the gifts that this little mind could imagine. I'd be distracted by the wind and by the birds, as to be drawn to nature.

"But mom, I still cannot see the angels," I would tell her.

"Be still, listen, and be present and you'll hear them, as they will whisper to you, stand up little girl, walk forward, and embrace what this life has to give you.

While these were not her exact words, that is what it said to me, and that thought has been a compass throughout my life.

Many times, I would reflect upon these words and these thoughts that I had as a child. I realize now, as an adult, I need to look back to see and appreciate all the journeying through all the different opportunities in my life. Each was a stepping stone through all the doors that the angels had prepared for me.

FEELING THE PRESENCE OF THE ANGELS

I was with my friend, Sharon, up at a camp they had a little ways out of town. It was afternoon, and we were lying on the bunk-beds just chatting back and forth with each other when all of a sudden, I felt a tingling all over my body. I could sense that there was a presence that was there with me; it was light, and it was gentle. Tears began flowing down my face as I felt this kind gentle presence around me. I knew at that moment, that all those times my mother told me that they were angels all around us, I was experiencing it in that very moment. To this day, I believe that that was the first real life awareness of the gift my mother had given me, the gift of feeling the presence of angels.

I grew up in a very small town of about 480 people. Like the town, our life was also very small indeed. We were surrounded by nature, and we had many joys from living in our outdoor environment. We could be found playing in the brooks and the streams and making rafts and floating down a small river, picking apples and taking a bite out of a crisp apple on a cool fall day. Simple pleasures that became simple treasures.

This was a time when children could ride their bikes for miles and miles and not worry about having the troubles that people seem to experience in this day and age. There was a freedom, and there was a gift that you could just embrace each day to enjoy what the good Lord had given you as a child and let your imagination flow... and that we did.

RESCUE AT THE RIVER

One afternoon, my girlfriend and I took our little brothers along with us on an adventure. We rode our bikes down to an area called the covered bridge. The water was high that spring, and as a couple of kids with a vivid imagination we had a desire to experience the stories we read in school of Tom Sawyer and Huckleberry Finn.

When the water rose, the wooden picnic tables that lined the riverbed would begin to float. Looking down from the window of the covered bridge, we saw that several of them were beginning to lift from the ground and they were bobbing along slowly on the edge of the river. We ran down to the disappearing river bank, with our little brothers in tow. We were about 11 or 12 at the time, and they were much younger.

We sought out to build a raft out of picnic tables that were next to the riverbank just like Tom Sawyer might do. Now mind you, we did not pay attention to the fast-moving water that was in the center of the river, or that many other picnic tables were floating and heading down river a bit quickly. We were only thinking of the exciting adventure that lay before us. So, we found some long poles that were branches that had broken off from the trees, and we proceeded to climb onto one of the picnic tables, pushing them further into the river as we edged it off the bank.

Now, being daring little children, and being very competitive, our little brothers decided they wanted to have their own raft and be like Tom Sawyer, too. We were too young to understand the science involved in this, and that the weight difference from us at our size to theirs would create different results. Our little brothers, with their light weight riding on the picnic table would mean they would move a lot faster than we would be going.

We started side-by-side, going along the edge of the water where the river was slow, with our poles pushing us along. Then, something very scary happened. As we got further out into the water, the flow of the water was getting faster and faster. Our little brothers were now moving away from us, and we were starting to lose control of being able to stay safely next to them. So, believe it or not, my girlfriend and I started jumping from one picnic table to another to get closer to where our little brothers were as they were flowing out towards the fast water. We could see they were getting scared too, as their eyes were getting bigger as they headed out towards the fast-moving water.

This is why I always say, I always have angels around me. As unbelievable as it sounds, we were able to jump over table after table to get close enough to them to jump onto their picnic table raft. Our added weight started to slow the table down, and taking our polls, we pushed hard against the bottom of the riverbed, pushing us all safely to the shallow water of the riverbank. We pulled our little brothers to safety, and held our dear little brothers who were crying by then.

They were so thankful that they were saved from the fast river water, and we gathered our bikes and made our way home. But there was one more thing we had to do. We knew we had to make a pact with them so that our parents would never find out how dangerous this whole situation was, so we all put our hands together and made a promise that we would never tell them how scary of a day we had on the Ellis River by the Covered Bridge, because isn't that is what Tom Sawyer and Huckleberry Finn would do.

Many times in my life I've had experiences where there's no question at all that I had help from heaven above. These types of experiences throughout my journey have created an imprint on my soul that have allowed me to help different people along the way. My life in the small town where I grew up is only part of the circumstances that made up my upbringing. I was a middle child and the girl in the crowd who didn't have a horse. There were many times I felt like I was on the outside looking in. My friends would all gather together, and I would help them with their horses and get everybody settled in their saddles only to wave goodbye to them as they rode away. My heart broke, wishing and hoping that I could actually be with them, or be even be invited along somehow. But it never happened. As I grew older, I learned in my later years that the joy that I had in helping them get ready to go on their adventures, and the joy that I had in hearing their stories when they came back was a true blessing. Those were with the gifts that I was able to participate in. I treasured the time I was able to brush the horses and get them ready to go on their journey.

Little did I know that this same pleasure was to be the gift in my life of having my own horse years later. In total, I have had the gift of having five different horses of my own, two of which were rescues. I have raised foals, trained horses in dressage, barrel racing, jumping and games. But my most pleasurable times has been when I was quietly being present with the horses, grooming them and having that relationship with them. The same gift that I had as a young girl getting the horses ready for their adventures with my friends. It is finding the joy in the simple gifts, to truly embrace life's gifts within our life story, that give us the tools to use later in life.

◈ ASK YOURSELF

Have you ever found yourself in a precarious situation and needed to be brave to make it through? What did that mean to you?

_____

_____

_____

What small things in life have blessed you, and have they changed to be something bigger than what you ever imagined?

_____

_____

_____

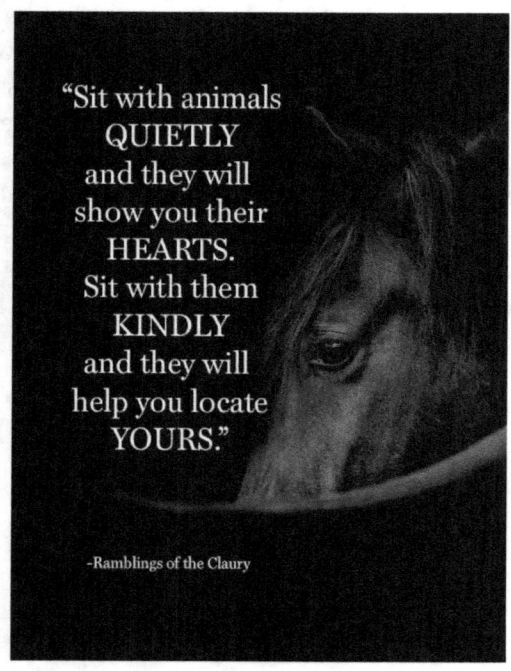

"Sit with animals
QUIETLY
and they will
show you their
HEARTS.
Sit with them
KINDLY
and they will
help you locate
YOURS."

-Ramblings of the Claury

OUR STEPPING STONES IN LIFE

As I reflect back to the different times and different experiences I had as a child, I realize just how important they became to me. I was able to use them in my management years and was able to use them even in raising my children. Each event became a stepping stone. To be able to embrace the different losses in life that we all go through and apply them to the path ahead as a lesson learned, and a path traveled, is the tapestry of our life.

I can remember, as a young girl, in the summer time, when my mother worked, I was not old enough to stay by myself, so I had the privilege of being able to go with my father each day as he went off to work. In his role as a game warden, he would leave each day to check on beaver dams and water levels in the lakes and even saving animals who were hurt.

Another important factor to know about life in those days, as far children were concerned, they were meant to be seen and not heard, and I was to join him for a whole day... Oh my, it was a little scary. I would gather the lunches that my mother had made for the both of us, and I would climb up into the truck and wait to see where it was that my father was taking me. I did so, quietly, mind you.

A Stream at Grafton Notch

One day, he drove towards the notch area; this is where he wanted to go and check on some fishing licenses. He had me bring along my fishing pole. He positioned me at a small pool in a little stream and he had me sit there and fish while he went upstream to check on some fisherman's license.

So, I sat there in the sunshine, threw my worm into the water, and I tried to catch the trout that I could see, as it was clear all the way to the bottom of the stream. As I was sitting there, suddenly, I heard quite the commotion in the distance. I looked down into the water and I started to see fish floating by on the surface of the water.

Then I heard the commotion come stumbling down the stream, as this man came running by me trying to elude my father! Obviously, he had caught too many fish, or perhaps did not have a fishing license at all! And then I looked up, and saw my father in the woods working his way toward me. He was smiling at me, and he said in his quiet way, "So, did you catch any fish?"

"No, I didn't catch any fish. But I did see some float by," I told him. "And then I saw a man go running by me, and boy, did he look as surprised to see me, as I was to see him!"

Dad smiled that sly smile of his and motioned to me to follow him. As we gathered up my fishing pole and fishing basket, we worked our way back to the truck. I thought to myself that my father never did anything that didn't have an intention behind it, and this taught me a couple of things. For one thing, make sure that you're following the rules, and know what it is that you're supposed to be doing or you could end up running down a brook one day, trying to escape from what it was you weren't supposed to be doing in the first place. The man who ran down that brook was long gone by the time we got back to the truck, but I had a feeling Dad knew who he was and, more than likely, unless he learned his lesson, he may see Dad again one day. Nothing is truly hidden when you're walking on the wrong side of the line of good and bad. One way or another, it will surface like Ivory Soap, as my Mom would say.

(For those of you that may not know what Ivory Soap does when it is in the water... it floats! You can't sink it as it pops right back up to the surface. So, Mom always said that one may think a fib is hidden under the surface... but it will end up floating like Ivory Soap. So, never tell a lie!)

THE DEVIL IS IN THE DETAILS

My father was a man who strove for perfection. We always had the prettiest lawns, our flowerbeds were always beautiful and pristine, our fence had the perfect line of grass along the bottom that my father would measure to make sure that it was a clean cut. If it wasn't, you would have to go back and fix it until it was right. In our garden, I would have to count every carrot to make sure that there was room for the other carrots to grow. And he would come out and check on it to make sure that I did it right. So, with all these lessons around me, I always made sure I paid attention to the details.

It is the details in our life, the small intricate details, that end up making up who we truly are as people. To some people, and even to myself, those years when I was young, I would think that he was being cruel. I thought that no other dad would make sure that every third carrot was pulled out, and then come out and make me repeat having to trim underneath the fence line to make sure that it was perfect, the way it needed to be.

But I ended up realizing, that all this teaching wound up helping me in my career in more ways than I can count. Being focused on the details taught me how to lead and coach people in my later years. Looking at the details that may make up a protocol or a policy that would inevitably keep someone safe, and then help teach other people how to apply those details turned out to be critical. I found that it came easy to me because it was part of my nature due to the lessons that my Dad taught me.

When I was young, having all these traits instilled in me, in trying to make sure everything was where it was supposed to be, that everything had a place, yes, it was complicated as a child and I'd become very frustrated. I didn't understand why I had to learn these things. I would retaliate against my father and complain to my mother, even to the point where I would get into trouble just to get out of having to do what it was that my father would ask me to do. Again, and again I would find myself running away from the teaching that was being placed before me, not understanding how invaluable those teachings were going to be to me in my later life.

I learned from my childhood, no matter what it was that I attempted to do, my father was teaching me to do it with pride; to take care of the things that you were able to have, and to consider it a privilege to be able to have those things. Whether it was a car, or a bike, or whatever it was that you'd earned, it was your duty to take care of the gifts you were given.

I realize now, that those values and traits of life have been the backbone to everything that I have done as I am reflecting back through my life's journey. So, as frustrating and cruel I thought it was as a child, it has become one of my biggest blessings, and I am so thankful my Dad was persistent. Treasure all that is before you and take nothing for granted. Each encounter, each opportunity, is a gift of learning and creates a memory. These are truly the steppingstones of your life.

LESSONS FROM MY CAMP ADVENTURES WITH DAD

My father would often take me to camp. He would take me on long walks with him through the woods, and along the path, he would find animal tracks and teach me each sign they left us. My father was a man of few words. I felt it was a privilege to be asked to be able to go with him. We would walk along, and I would pay careful attention watching for his hands to signal to the left or to the right pointing out different mosses on the rocks. He might point to a tree or something that he wanted me to see to teach me about the different leaves on the types of trees, and he would say, "Remember to keep your head up so that you can see what it is that is around you."

As a child, I learned from these walks about all the different types of mosses, and he would teach me which type of moss I could use to help heal a cut and which type of moss that I could actually eat. There were many things in the forest that I would learn on those quiet walks at camp. He would show me the different animal signs as we were walking along down by the lake.

One day in particular stands out in my memory of those walks. On that day, my father took out a jackknife and said that we were going to go over to a spruce tree as he wanted me to try something. "You see this knot that is here?" he asked. "I'm going to cut this piece off, and I want you to put it in your mouth and start chewing it." One thing that I learned as a kid was that I would just do whatever it was that my dad told me to do without question. So, I put that sticky piece of pitch, (which it smelled like) into my mouth, and I started chewing on it. The more that I chewed it, the more that it turned into a gum-like consistency... I'm not sure if it was very good for a child's teeth, but believe it or not, it did turn into Spruce gum! All the while, he had that knowing grin and was aware that I wasn't a true fan of the taste, but he was tickled that I stuck it out and turned it into gum without a fight.

◇ ASK YOURSELF:

Have you ever had to "trust" someone even though you had no idea how things might end up by doing so?

_____

_____

_____

Did you find it hard to muster up the courage to have that trust and did you work your way through it?

_____

_____

_____

Another day at camp, Dad got his boat ready for my little brother and I, and he sent us out early in the morning to go fishing all by ourselves. Boy, did I feel grown up! We headed out into a little cove by the camp, loaded our worms onto our hooks, dropping our sinkers to the bottom of the lake. All of a sudden, my brother shouted, I've got something!" The way he brought it up from the bottom, it looked like he must have gotten his line caught on a branch... but then he pulled it up, and there, on the end of the line, was a black fish with a big fat head! It wasn't the prettiest fish, and because of that, I didn't dare touch it! So, we maneuvered the boat to shore and ran up to the camp with that funny looking fish on the end of the line. We were cheering loudly as we ran up the path, "We got something!!" We went running onto the porch and Dad came out to see what we were hollering about.

"What is it?" I asked my father. He smiled at us and said, "Breakfast!" My brother and I just looked at each other not understanding how anyone could eat such an ugly looking fish. Come to find out, it was a "hornpout" or a catfish that lives down in the leaves in the dark bottom waters. It is also delicious and was one of my Dad's favorite fish to eat.

An important thing to know about this fish is that those spine barbs in the front of the fish by their mouth are very sharp!! It is known to cut a fisherman's hands and can cause quite an infection. Thank goodness, with our excitement, and because it was not a pretty thing to touch, we didn't get close to its mouth and did not get hurt by this ugly fellow. Dad grabbed the line and used his gloves to show us how to take the hornpout off the line so as to not get cut. I say it was my angel that kept me from touching it, and maybe that the good Lord made it look this way, so kids ran with it on the line instead of touching it. We all tried a piece of the fish that Mom fried up in the iron skillet at camp, and you know... it really did taste good!!!

Hornpout fish

One of the other things that we always did when we went on our walks, it began with him telling me to grab a cup, or a little tin pail with a handle. As we walked along, we would pick berries to take back to Mom so that she could make us pancakes or muffins with the fresh berries that we gathered during our walk.

One time, when we were on our walk, all of a sudden, my father stopped and motioned to me to stand still. Little did I know that from his view, he was seeing a mama bear and her cubs that were up ahead enjoying the raspberry bushes. He swung his hands backwards at me telling me to go back down the path that we had just come from. He didn't tell me until I got back to camp why we had to turn around. I believe that was a very smart decision on his part. Being a little girl, I may have startled the mama bear by screaming, and that type of excitement none of us needed, even the bears!

My father had great respect and honor for native American traditions, and I am very grateful that he has passed this down to me. I have always felt that there is a message hidden in a visit from an animal, or standing in a grove of hemlock trees listening to the wind in their branches. There has always been an awareness, a grounding sort of connection to them in some way. I believe it is from being taught to respect nature and protect it, that my father instilled in me since I was a little girl.

There is a book called *Animal Speaks* written by Ted Andrews that I have always enjoyed reading. In it he says,

> *"And with it all, I am always amazed at the wonder of nature, its multiplicity, and especially at what it is saying to me about my own life at the time of such encounters. I look for what it is trying to teach me. I know nature speaks to us if we listen. Every animal has a story to tell. Every flower blossoms with reminders to be creative, and every tree whispers with its rustling leaves the secrets of life."*

This insight reminds me of all the conversations that I once had with my father as a young girl.

◇ ASK YOURSELF

What experiences have you had as a child where you learned to stay away from something, and how did it help you in later years in life?

_____

_____

_____

What lessons did you learn?

_____

_____

_____

ARE THINGS REALLY WHAT WE PERCEIVE?

On another one of our adventures, we packed up our lunch and took a drive early in the morning to a place called Grafton Notch. Dad knew of all these places along the roads where there were ponds and all kinds of streams that had beaver dams, which were all the things that he needed to check on.

During this particular adventure, Dad pulled over to the side of the road and stopped the truck. Now mind you, I've learned the gift of being able to go with my Dad is that it helps to be very quiet and do as you're told. Dad looked over to me and grabbed his green game warden's backpack and said, "Time to get out, we've got to go over there through that trail." So, I clamored out of the truck and began looking around but I didn't see a trail.

Dad came from behind the truck, looked at me and just shook his head, smiled and said, "Follow me." He pushed back a large Alder bush and behold... behind it was this old tote road that we started to walk down. It was a beautiful trail, and Dad and I walked probably a good two miles. As we walked through a grove of trees, I started to see this beautiful pond ahead of us. We walked over to the shore and Dad pointed over to some bushes that were on the shore of the pond.

Grafton Notch

"Go over and get that canoe ready," he told me.

I looked around and I didn't see any canoe on the shore.

"We're going to take the canoe over to the other side of the pond," he said, pointing to a spot across the pond. "I have to check on a beaver dam." Sure enough, as I went over to the pile of brush that Dad told me to move, there was this Old Town canoe laying under the bushes. It was kept there so that he could use it to go out and check on the dam.

Dad and I got into the canoe, and we made our way out across this gorgeous pond. It was quiet, and there was a hue across the water like sea smoke. We went over to the beaver dam, and Dad checked to see if he needed to come back and take care of it, but it all seemed fine. Dad also brought along some fishing poles, and they looked a little different than the fishing poles I was used to. These were very long and thin, and they had a different type of reel. The fishing line he used with the fishing pole seemed a little different as well. Dad pulled a little tin out of his game warden pack, and he opened it. It had the most beautiful looking fishing flies—some that he had made himself and some that he had received from a few of his friends.

All of a sudden it dawned on me, *Dad's gonna teach me how to fly fish! Or at least I'm gonna be able to watch him fly fish!* Dad set up the pole, and he started to show me how to whip the line over the top of my head and lay it out onto the water so that the fish could come up to the top of the water and grab the fly. I will never forget the sound as that line went back and forth across over the top of Dad's head. It was so graceful, and it was laid out like a feather on top of the water.

Sure enough, something came up and bumped it! So, Dad reeled in the line and asked me to come over to where he was sitting. He placed his hand over the top of mine and took my arm and went back and forth to dry the line above our head and laid it on top of the water. Time after time, he showed me how to dry the line over my head so that the fly would land lightly on the water.

Finally, the time came when I was given the pole, and Dad had me do it by myself. I laid the fly on top of the water and right as the fly hit the top of the water, a big splash happened! I was so excited, and Dad was excited too!

He said to me, "Keep the line tight, let him go, reel it in." "Boy, it's a big fish!"

I exclaimed to him, "Oh my goodness, what is it?"

He smiled, looked at me and said, "That's supper!!"

"TIME WITH DAD"

I will forever treasure that day. We did take the fish home, and Mom cooked it up for us for supper. If memory serves me right, it was a big brown trout. To this day, I still have not caught another one.

But I did have an occasion, later on in my years, when I was going through an antique shop in Camden Maine that something amazing happened. I came upon this gorgeous picture that someone had painted, it was a watercolor print. It was the exact replica of that moment, where a man and his daughter are out in a canoe on a pond, with a haze across the pond, and it looked exactly as the vision in my memory.

"Time With Dad"

It was hard for me to imagine that what I was seeing was real. Then I saw title of the picture, it was named *"Time with Dad."* I gasped and started to cry. It brought back all those memories of that wonderful day that I spent with dad. I truly believe that it was a gift from dad sent from heaven, so that I could always remember that moment when I caught that big brown trout on the day that we walked through a path that no one would've ever seen to check on a beaver dam, to use a canoe that no one would ever find, and to teach a little girl her first fly fishing lesson.

Again, there are angels amongst us, as my mom would say. So, take those moments to stop and pause. Listen to that inner voice to help you experience such gifts as these. I get to visit this memory every time I pass the picture in my hallway named, *Time with Dad.*

◇ ASK YOURSELF:

Have you ever received the unexplainable gift of a memory from years ago?

_____

_____

_____

Has this experience opened your eyes to look for more opportunities to receive such gifts?

_____

_____

_____

The "Runner Who Never Ran"

THE GIFT OF JOURNALING

As I became a little older, and my handwriting was legible, Dad would have me write from his journal that he would do every day after a day's work. You see, they must record the events of a game warden's day as a matter of record.

When he would return home from his day's work, he would write it all down into a journal in his office. All the years that Dad served within the warden's service are recorded in these journals for his entire 27 years of service.

One of the things that Dad did was that he would take that record and create a duplicate so that he had his own personal journals as a replica of his life as a game warden. Now that I was older, he would have me copy the journal into his private collection so that he didn't have to do it. He would smile at me and say, "It's one of the benefits of having a kid that has good handwriting."

So after the dishes were done, he would have me sit at his beautiful old desk that was in his office, and I would transcribe his journal of that day and put it into his personal journals; it was here that I would learn of his day.

Below is an actual entry from Dad's Journal from 1969 in the State's Archives:

WARDEN JOHN SWASEY, ANDOVER: PEOPLE SEEM TO BE GREATLY CONCERNED ABOUT THE DEER THIS WINTER. "SO MUCH SNOW THAT THE DEER CAN'T GET AROUND AND ARE STARVING." I HAD OCCASION TO GO INTO AN AREA WHERE THERE WAS SOME PULP CUTTING TAKING PLACE, WITH A SMALL DEER YARD NEARBY. THE MAN DOING THE CUTTING CALLED AND SAID THERE WAS A DEER STAYING IN HIS CUTTINGS WITH ONE FRONT LEG BADLY INJURED. HE SAID THE DEER WAS HAVING A HARD TIME GETTING ABOUT IN THE SNOW AND WANTED TO KNOW IF I COULD USE A DART GUN AND TRANQUILIZE HIM AND REMOVE THE LEG. I WENT TO THE LOCATION AND STARTED UP INTO THE HAULING ROADS. AS I GOT UP CLOSE TO THE YARD, I SAW A DEER FEEDING ON A TOP AND AS I APPROACHED, IT MOVED OUT AHEAD OF ME. I NOTICED IT WAS THE DEER WITH THREE LEGS. AS I STARTED TO CIRCLE AHEAD OF THE DEER, I FOUND, LYING IN THE TRAIL, THE LOWER PART OF ITS LEG. IT APPEARED TO HAVE DROPPED OFF THE NEIGHT BEFORE, IT SEEMS TO ME IF A THREE-LEGGED DEER CAN SURVIVE A WINTER SUCH AS THIS THAT A HEALTHY, FOUR-LEGGED ONE SURELY CAN. THE SNOW AT THIS TIME MEASURED 54 INCHES IN THE SOFTWOOD. THE DEER WAS SINKING ABOUT 13 INCHES.

I think back now to the gift I had of being able to read about all of the things that he did throughout the day. The interaction with nature with the duties of a game warden as they take care of the forest, the fish, and the animals included stories of otters and moose, and of an injured loon that he brought home one time while it healed. There were names of ponds, camps and of people that he had interacted with throughout his day.

I can remember one time when Dad received a call that he had to go to court because some guy had been arrested. This man told the arresting officer that he was with a game warden by the name of John Swasey on the day in question. So, his defense to the detective was he must be mistaken regarding his involvement in the crime.

On the day of the court hearing, the State presented my father's journal that had been recorded and sent to the State. It presented evidence saying that my father was in a totally different location than the one the man who was arrested was saying he was that day. The defending attorney for the man who had been arrested stated, "This must be a mark-up, because he wasn't there. The defendant was in a different location with that Game Warden." Little did the attorney know of the duplicate journal that my father kept in his office. And the interesting thing was, that the location could not be disputed, because the writing in this journal was in my handwriting, and not in my father's! So, the defending attorney could not say that my father had mocked up this document, as it was in a different handwriting all together, mine!

I'll never forget Dad coming home and sharing that story at the supper table. And me sitting there thinking, there's a young girl's handwriting that was presented at court today to defend my father and to make the truth be told of where that man was on that day in question. I can remember my father saying that the judge said to the man who had been arrested, "I believe you chose the wrong Game Warden to be the one to try to get you off from this charge."

I bet Dad was not used as a scapegoat again, at least not to my knowledge!!

◈ ASK YOURSELF

Have you ever experienced a point in your life when something in your past changed someone else's life?

_____

_____

_____

How do you reflect on this now?

_____

_____

_____

The "Runner Who Never Ran"

EMBRACING THE MOMENT

There were many stories that Dad would share at the supper table. We always called it supper and not dinner back then, at least at our house. I would come home from school and start the potatoes at 4 p.m. so we could eat between 5-5:30 p.m. Mom worked until 4:30 p.m. at the local wood products running a ripsaw. It was hard work and scary at times... (that story comes next.)

We were all sitting around the supper table and Dad said that he went to check on a beaver dam that day. It was winter, and back then, we had plenty of snow to snowshoe through. Dad said that as he approached the area, he heard a lot of chatter and scurrying around. As he crouched down by an ole cedar tree, he watched six otters sliding down the embankment like a bunch of kids, and then scurrying around with each other like they were wrestling and repeating the action again and again.

Dad said he didn't have the heart to disturb them, so he went back to the truck instead of pulling the limbs out of the dam, or for that fact, looking to see if it needed to be blown up!! Yes, they used to do that! I remember close calls being bantered back and forth between him and his partner about whose turn was it to blow up the next beaver dam. If I am not mistaken, it was dynamite, which stands to reason why Dad would always say..."Don't go messing around in my truck." He and his partner would argue about where it should be placed and who did what better. All in good fun, and no one got hurt, even the beavers... they sure did have some amazing experiences blowing up those beaver dams!!

This taught me to look at the circumstances and to examine my surroundings, before becoming just task minded. He took the moment to enjoy the beauty of those otters having fun. He honored them by not disturbing their moment of frolic. This lesson taught me to stop and be present in the moment. Listen, look, and absorb the gifts before you. Just because you have an agenda to attend to, you sometimes need to stop and alter the course.

As a manager in assisted living communities, I always told my staff, when they were in a flutter about a task that needed to be done immediately. I would say... "Is it on fire? Will someone get hurt or not receive the necessary care if you stop for that moment and listen to the story that you may have heard one hundred times before?"

In a business like ours, of assisted living communities, it is important to take the time to honor those who you are taking care of and listen to that story that is so important to them. It is never wasted time, even though it is a juggle with so many people to take care of and with not enough hands to do the job. Taking the moment to embrace the memory is the priority, and it's essential as it honors a person's journey, and who knows, you may hear a story of a playful otter or two, or how someone blew up a beaver dam with dynamite!!

◇ ASK YOURSELF:

How can you be more present in your life?

_____

_____

_____

How often do you put away all devices and allow yourself to be in the moment wherever you are?

_____

_____

_____

Andover Wood Products Annual Picnic

Annual Picnic

Mom working at Andover Wood Products

PERSEVERANCE

My mom worked at a sawmill that made products for Ethan Allen. It was a great little mill nestled in the western mountains of Maine. My older brother worked there, and I had my first "punch the clock" job there too. It was the staple to the townsfolks, and they created amazing beautiful pieces for Ethan Allen.

We had community BBQ picnics at the Lovejoy Covered Bridge every summer, and boy, was that chicken good! This event was the mark of the mill's two-week vacation that everyone was able to take, as the mill would shut down for those two weeks every year. Everyone would jump into their vehicles and pile into the back of their pickups with all the kids and down to the field we would have BBQ chicken, corn, rolls, and salad. What a wonderful way to start your vacation because it was lots of fun!

Mom ran a piece of equipment called a rip saw. This was a dangerous job and you had to be quick, have a keen eye, and be in sync with the person on the other end of the saw. Watching them work the wood was like the ebb and flow of the ocean, back and forth so smoothly, cutting all the knots out of the different types of wood.

One day, my mother was working the saw and it kicked back, hard. The board splintered into pieces and had slung back towards mom like a bullet from a gun. But mom, with her keen eye and reflexes, put her hand up, and it went right through her hand from her pinky finger right through to the pointer finger and it came out the other side. My brother was there that day and had to help cut off the long end of the board so they could take her to hospital in the next town over.

WOMEN ARE employed as rip-saw helpers and lumber inspectors. Their speed and keen eyesight make them ideal for these jobs.

Just hearing the story again makes my hand hurt. I remember my brother sharing that it was one of the hardest things he ever had to do was to cut that board as he knew it was hurting Mom, but he knew they had to get her to the hospital, so he just did it.

Sometimes we are placed in circumstances that no one ever wants to be in, but we are there for a reason. By having my brother so close by, it helped my mom to realistically have use of her hand. Making those tough decisions, like what Mom did to stop that board, saved it from going right through her, or someone else.

It was a long road for Mom with that hand after that incident with the rip saw. It was even sadder that it was hard for her to decorate the cakes that she would make for our friends at local events like the governor's inaugural event at the Balsams or for weddings all around the area. My mother had a talent that was beyond words. She would take a thimble-looking object with a flat top and twirl it between her thumb and pointer finger and create these amazing looking doves with a squirt of the frosting bag. I would sit there and watch her, hoping that one didn't come out right, just so she would take it off and give me the frosting! She made roses that looked real and created figures out of frosting that hardened to give dimensional appearances on the side of a cake. They were a work of art.

She had such a signature effect on her work that people would say, "That must be a cake made by Jean Swasey!" They were beautiful. Mom had a hard time continuing the same amount of work on her cakes after the incident with the rip saw. I knew it was sad for her and painful when she would try to do some here or there. She had an artistic ability and an eye to create an image out of frosting like wood carvers did. And speaking of wood carving, she mastered this as well, using balsam wood.

◈ ASK YOURSELF:

Have you ever been in a position when you had to persevere through a tough situation?

_____

_____

_____

If so, would you do anything different now knowing the out-come?

_____

_____

_____

THE ART OF ILLUSION

Balsam wood and the smell of paint and glue, that was often our kitchen table in the evening. Dad had a passion for HO trains. An HO train is a modeling scale of 1:87 to scale, and it is noted to be the most popular model railroad used in the world.

Dad had transformed half of the basement in our house into train yards, towns, logging roads, churches, and even accidents on the paved like roads. He had bridges, railway stations with working lights and train trestles that were scattered strategically throughout. We had even tunnels going through a replica of a local mountain in town.

I remember mom and dad working into the night painting little figurines of men, women, and children; they looked so real with perfect era clothes and tools in hand. There were matchbox cars on paved roads with working crossing lights for when a train would come through. Telephone poles with working lights had telephone wires strung from pole to pole. They even created a replica of our little western town right down to the church, our house, and the mountains that surrounded us. A mural was all along the back wall over septic pipes and plumbing that you had to look closely to see that it was even there.

One of the roads was always a mystery to me as a child. If you looked at the road from different spots within the working railyards, it always looked like was going straight away from you. You could crawl under the trainyard and pop up in a hole cut to access an area on the track. From there, you could help a train that jumped the track, or just work on a project build. This one special road, no matter what point I looked at it from, always looked like it was taking me out of town. The road always followed you, so I could imagine taking a trip as it went out of town to the mountains. Dad would smile when I would pop from hole to hole looking at the road or show a friend in amazement. I would say, "Now you see that road right there, now look at it from over here. It will always look like it is heading away from you."

Later in years, I learned it was because of an optical illusion as they had used balsam wood and created some the of the buildings protruding out from the wall. It looked like it was a whole building or store, but it was only about one-half of an inch thick, the rest was how it was painted in the mural. People would come to the house just to see the trains and to have Dad work the control station where he had at least three, if not more, command controls to run multiple trains at once. Sometimes Dad would let us kids push the button to blow the horns on the train; it was quite a thrill!

Andover General Store

* * * * * * * * * * *

Laser-cut wood w/ peel and stick parts.
Includes 'steel roof, plastic chimney, plastic windows
and details, and etched brick foundation.
Footprint: 3" x 7 3/4"

* * * * * * * * * * *

Mount Blue Model Co.
P.O. Box 460
White Horse Beach, MA 02381
www.mountbluemodelco.com

Our basement was a whole other world with figurine people going here and there. You would see rescue trucks assisting an accident on the side of the mountain as Dad had a matchbox vehicle melted and distorted by baking it in the oven, with tires and debris laying along the roadway. You would see a person lying in the road and a rescue worker helping them.

Logging trucks with real logs were on their trailers going up the logging roads to a working yard where they were to be delivered to the train yard. An actual crane took logs off a truck and trailer to load onto the train bed. It was truly an amazing work of art and imagination. In case you are interested, I have included this link as it will take you to a kit that has a replica of an ole general store from that small western town where Dad's trains once worked. These types of structures were built by skillful hands and painted to be replicas of a point in time. It created many memories of yesteryear all through imagination and artistic talent. https://seaportmodelworks.com/product/1017-h/

◈ ASK YOURSELF:

Have you ever experienced an optical illusion?

_____

_____

_____

Can you look at something in your life from a different perspective?

_____

_____

_____

How does that change what you thought to be true?

_____

_____

_____

The Art of Illusion

Wardens and biologists kept a sharp watch on snow depths in deer wintering areas. Warden Alden Kennett, Bethel, and John Swasey, Andover, found near-record depths in many areas.

CAUGHT RED-HANDED

I have had the gift of other people reaching out to share a story or two about my Dad. There is one gal that I grew up with who is a natural storyteller. She shared this story she called, "The younger days and Andover's law of the jungle!"

A young man with a couple of guys jacked a deer. Jacking a deer is hunting it out of season or at night. The young man instructed one of the younger men to be sure to clean out the trunk of the vehicle to make sure all the blood and hair was gone from the jacked deer they shot that day.

The next day, who but my dad knocked on their door. No one could figure out how he would have known, but there was the game warden, my dad, at their door! It was said that dad had an inkling about hunting not being done in season. So, dad politely asked to see this young man's car trunk. The young man began to pray, "Oh God, please let so and so who cleaned the trunk to have done a good job!"

So, with baited breath, he opened the trunk. Let's just say there was no need for forensics... hair and blood was everywhere. So, Dad collected the deer meat that this man had hid and went on his way. Then, a week later, it was hunting season. Dad drove by the same house and there was a nice buck hanging there, one of those that would make the "over 200 pounds club" deer.

Dad thought for sure it must be the young man's father's deer. So, Dad knocked on the door once again.

He asked, "Whose deer is that?"

The young man answered the door and piped up all proud and honest, "It's mine! It's a big one too! Should hit the over 200-pound club!" (Mind you, he had not gone to court yet, so he wasn't supposed to be hunting.)

Dad just shook his head and laughed as the young man realized what he just blurted out. Now some people might have been mad, but dad knew it was just a proud kid being happy he had shot a big buck. To this day, that same young man, now pushing 70 will tell you, "That John Swasey was one heck of a game warden!"

There were many a story that people would share. One was about a guy that was back in the woods during hunting season on a cool, sunny day. He found a nice tree to lean against to sit in the sun and wait for the sun to start to go down to see if a deer would come out at dusk.

He had his eyes closed with his rifle across his knees when he heard beside him, "How's the hunting?" He said he about jumped out of his skin! There, sitting beside him, was my dad! He never heard him approach or even sit down! This type of story was told by a many a hunter, and I can remember they would say that they never knew when my dad would show up! They said, "He sure kept me honest!"

◈ ASK YOURSELF:

Have you ever stepped over the line or broke a rule but are in some way proud of it?

_____

_____

_____

The "Runner Who Never Ran"

DOING THE UNSEEN AND ADD A LITTLE LAUGHTER

Growing up, where people would say to me, later in life, "Did you know that your father used to drop off a deer that had been shot so that my brothers and I could have venison for supper?" My dad knew which people were struggling in town, and when he caught a poacher poaching deer, he would take that meat and deliver it to the family in need. He would do the same thing when he caught someone in a closed brook that you weren't supposed to be smelting in. He would deliver those smelts to those people in need. I guess I became a continuance of my father and making sure that I take care of those who are in need, as I believe he passed on that passion in me.

They also passed onto me the gift of looking at the lighter side of life. Creating joy is one of the traits I believed my mother passed down to me. You see, my mother had a great sense of humor, and she had the capability of being able to put together a really good prank.

One day, before my father was heading off to work, he told us that he had to go check on a closed smelting brook that evening that was closed off from smelting. The smelts were running so much that the brook actually looked black with smelts.

Little did he know that my mother and her friend had planned a little prank for him and his partner, Alden. My mother and her friend had decided that they were going dress up as men, so they put on old clothes and a big hat and tucked their hair up underneath their hats.

They took poles that they cut the ends off and took off to that brook after dark where my father and his partner were going to be watching to see if anybody was smelting that night. As my father and his partner Alden came to the brook, they had their flashlights and they aimed them down on these two men who had their poles down into this closed brook where they were not supposed to be fishing. They told these two men to take their poles out of the water, which they believed had nets on the end of them to catch the smelts. The two men didn't do what they were told.

Dad became pretty angry, and proceeded to go down to the brook to escort them out of the brook. As he went to reach for the man, mom and her friend started laughing, "Oh, we're not fishing, John!"

Now mind you, they probably were having fun planning this little escapade and may have had a sip or two as they were preparing for the evening. If I remember the story right, they were laughing so hard that my father and Alden had to help them up from the brook. And if my memory serves me correctly, my father was not too happy, especially when he got back to the vehicle and saw that it had a flat tire and he had to change it. He had to drive them home due to that sip or two they had while waiting for dad and Alden to show up.

Many times, this story was told in my childhood days and we all would laugh about how dad had been pranked by mom and her friend. Pranks were something that happened around our household, so you always took care to look at your environment, not knowing what you might be getting yourself into.

◇ ASK YOURSELF:

Have you ever pulled a prank or practical joke?

_____

_____

_____

Has one been pulled on you?

_____

_____

_____

What was the result?

_____

_____

_____

There is a lot of history that can be accessed about the Game Warden Service in the 40s-60s. These pictures from 1969 are from a great magazine called, *Maine Fish and Game*.

Back then, there was a large focus on the sportsman field in Maine. The wardens would ride their snowmobile to remote camps and check on them for snow load on their roofs, as we had a lot of snow during those years. As you can see, this camp didn't make out very well. We would always ride into a camp that we used to call C Pond camp and have to shovel the roof off or it could have ended up looking like this one! These archives can be found on the web if you want to read more stories of yesteryear, a wonderful piece of our history in Maine.

Wardens were busy long into the spring checking camps while on patrol. Warden Chick Howe, Greenville, found several whose owners did not respond to the warnings in time.

UP AND ADAM...

Time to Go to Work!

I can remember when I was about 15 years old, during the summertime, and I would get on my bike in the morning around 8 o'clock and I'd ride about two and half miles to the river to a place called Flat Rocks, where I would wash my hair in the river's pool. To this day, I can remember how cold the water was, so cold that it would take my breath away. But it was worth it, because on my way home, after riding my bike, my long hair would be so soft from the water of that crystal clear brook. And believe you me, it sure woke you up for the day!

After getting home and having breakfast, I would gather my things and I would once again ride my bike another three miles to a place up towards North Andover. This is where I worked as a bookkeeper doing payroll for a company that had a logging operation. I would work that job until about 11:30 a.m., and then the owner would have me go out to the garage and I would actually sharpen the chipper blades that would be shredding the logs for his logging operation. It was there that I learned how to operate a lathe.

I think of this today, and I am amazed that I was given that type of responsibility of doing payroll and taking care of some family's income, and then going out and working with those four-foot chipper blades on a water-injected lathe as a 15-year-old girl. Thinking of it now, that was a lot of responsibility for a young girl, but I loved it!

Later in the afternoon, I would travel back to the house to grab lunch and then get prepared to go work at an ice cream shop at three in the afternoon. I would work in the ice cream shop until 7 p.m. and then I would ride my bike to meet my friends and enjoy the rest of the evening.

Growing up in a very small community, where the town had a population of just over 400, the townspeople took care of each other, and it was nothing for me to just ride my bike from one location to another. Back in those years in that part of Maine, in the 1960s and 70s, things were very safe.

I learned from my father and my mother who both were hard workers that if I wanted something in life, I had to earn it. So, by having these multiple jobs, I had a goal in mind that I was going to be getting myself a new bike the following year, and being 16, I was going to be able to work at the Andover Wood products for my very first real job where I had to clock in. I did save up that money, and I did buy myself a new bike to be able to go to work the first time in an actual employment environment.

I ended up working four 10-hour days at the age of 16, and when my paycheck came, I had to give a portion to my father. I remember how proud I was getting my first check from the mill. Standing there looking at it and reading all the categories on the pay stub, I sensed my dad by my side.

He looked at me and asked, "Is that your first check?"

I replied, "Yes, my very first one."

He said, "How much are you giving your mother from your check?"

I just looked at him. I had no idea that I was supposed to give some of my check to Mom. At the time, I thought that it was mean to make me do that, but later I reflected on all the times I would ride with Mom to get groceries and when we got out to the car, Mom would start crying as she spent most of the money that week on food and how was she going to make payments on the things that needed to be paid. It wasn't till later years that I truly understood how that little bit of help made a difference.

Dad taught me that by contributing to the budget, it made things a little easier on mom because at that time, you needed to help your family and help bring the groceries in the front door.

◈ ASK YOURSELF:

What was your first real job?

_____

_____

_____

How did you spend your money? Did you save any or spend it as you earned it?

_____

_____

_____

If you could go back in time, what would you tell your young-er self to do with the money?

_____

_____

_____

Grandpa Heggeman (Mom's dad)

MY RELATION TO MY LINEAGE

've always had a passion for old books and to learn about yesteryear. I have the gift of having several of my family's old books from the 1800s, which lead me to learn more about my heritage.

As I was researching our family history, I found out that there was a lineage there that I didn't realize, people that were attorneys, accountants, medical doctors, law professors and other professionals in the medical field. They were deans of colleges, such as Boston College, that I would have not known were there until my daughter found this by researching our family history. She was able to search back to the 1500s on both sides of our family tree through her grandparents. There, she found stories of professionals who helped heal people, people who created laws, and then taught these skills as professors.

This lineage became my tapestry, my background, deep within my soul that helped me navigate my trails in life. As my mother shared all these life skills years ago, these became my angels to help me navigate the road ahead. That small voice that whispers in my ear, the interconnections that I had within my mind, body and my soul. Maybe this was the root of my desire to work in the medical field, and to help create regulations that support the needs of the people and the staff. I also had this deep desire to honor the land, to find minerals and learn about gemstones. I wanted to learn how these minerals were formed and what was in the layers of the earth that created them. One of these gifts I believe comes from my maternal grandfather.

The gift that I have from my mother's father was around how he loved the Midwest. He had the most amazing collection of arrowheads that he found while exploring Missouri. You see, Missouri was the land that his parents settled in when they came here during wartime from Europe. He grew up in the Midwest, and when we did the family history tree on my mother's side, we were able to identify all those years that took place during that time. It was so heartwarming learning about how my grandfather came to this country and to imagine those times and how hard it must have been trying to leave Europe during the war.

All I remember is how gentle and kind he was and how tall he was! My tall grandfather with a bright smile always wore a Stetson hat that he would let me try on as I sat in his lap. He would share stories with me of working on the railroad, his trips out west to his beautiful Midwest, and how he loved it there. His smile would beam as he spoke of how he would go and search for the arrowheads and how he admired the Native Americans and how talented they were in carving these arrowheads to survive. He had them displayed on black velvet so you could see each intricate curve in bone, and it was all behind glass to preserve them. Oh how I loved listening to his stories.

◈ ASK YOURSELF:

Have you looked back through your heritage and considered how it affected your future and your life?

_____

_____

_____

STARTING MY JOURNEY IN HEALTHCARE

My journey in assisted living (AL) started when I was driving a tractor to my neighbor's house to deliver them food in the winter in the early 1980s. I moved from that to being a cook in a small facility in southern Maine, to owning my own facility, and then to became an Executive Director for the assisted living division for Kindred Healthcare which included six AL facilities. This journey came with many joys and hardships along the way which were all lessons learned to pave my path for each turn in the river of life.

There was one time when I first started working in the healthcare industry as a cook in a small facility. Mind you, this was a big step for small town girl to step out and be responsible for the meals for all those wonderful residents... boy, was I nervous. So, as you can imagine, those residents taught me! They shared recipes, told stories, and encouraged me to pursue my desire to serve in that industry.

One day, there was a staff call out, and they needed someone to help the residents get ready for the day, so they asked if I would come and help. Of course, I did; these were my friends now, and I couldn't let them not receive help. They handed me these stockings for a dear lady who had very swollen legs. I knew they must have hurt as they were swollen and had a blue hue. When

I walked into her room, I looked at those small stockings and I looked at her legs, and I had no idea to how they would ever go on those legs. The resident noticed my perplexed look and smiled, "No worries, dearie, I'll talk you through it!" And so she did... this was the start of my healthcare career. Residents teaching me and this pattern continued throughout the next 30 years. The message is in the details!!

By then, I had three little girls of my own, and they would come to work with me sometimes. They would skip around and help the residents put puzzles together and sing with them, bringing the light of a child into the room.

One gentleman was 101 years old, and the girls would love to sit and hear his stories. He was a tall man, and they would giggle as I would put my thumb up to check his plumb line to make sure his hips were in alignment so he wouldn't hurt his back.

One day, while we were visiting, we spoke of how my grandfather on my mother's side used to work the railroad. The nice man asked me what his name was as he worked at the railroad too. Come to find out, this man had been my grandfather's boss on the railway!! We heard many a story of how my grandfather worked at the railroad station in Portland, Maine. He spoke of how he always loved it when my grandfather would bring his daughter with the long red hair to work with him; that young girl was my mom! He would share how he remembered her beautiful, long red curly hair.

Now, as this man laid in bed, he had the gift of having my grandfather's great, great grandchildren sitting on his bed. These three little girls, all with curly long hair, and two of them, identical twins, with the same red curly hair that my mother had. Imagine the memories this sparked for him! Tears rolled down his eyes the first time he saw them, and he looked up at me and said they had the same hair as my mother did all those years ago.

He shared with my daughters and I those stories of my grandfather that I would've never known, if it hadn't been for being in that place at that point in time, and I would have never known unless I had taken that job as a cook. Angels at work, I say, as this brought so much joy to the 101-year-old man. He would share about all the trips up to Mt. Washington on the railway and the trips to Boston and the snow they encountered in those years. He had pictures of the trains my grandfather worked on and where my mother played in the box cars and caboose.

BUILDING THE FOUNDATION

I worked as a cook in a little 36-bed facility in southern Maine for about eight months before I decided that it was time to continue my desire to become a nurse. I started by going to Southern Maine Technical College, SMTC as it was called at that time, and I attained my Certified Nursing Assistant (CNA) certificate. This was part of the educational path in my process to get my license as a Licensed Practical Nurse (LPN).

As I was working as a CNA within this same facility where I worked as a cook, my desire to become an LPN then changed. I realized I had a strong desire to be in an administrative role. I had a passion to support the staff who were taking care of the residents within the facility. I believed I could make changes that would affect the policies that ran these buildings. I wanted to create operational guidelines that supported the hands that took care of the residents.

I attained my Certified Residential Medication Aide (CRMA) certificate, so that I could learn how to dispense medications and learn how the different types of medications that the residents were being prescribed were helping them. Being a CNA/ CRMA, I could understand the role better and support their role throughout my career.

This small facility was one that had an owner who, in a word, was not ethical, and was quite cruel to his employees. At first, he didn't show up very often but things changed. I showed up to work one morning and found the housekeeper crying in the stairwell. I knew she was a very proud woman, and as I approached her, I knew that she would be hesitant to share with me why she was crying. So, I sat down beside her and asked if there was something that I could do for her.

Come to find out, the owner, who was up from Florida, had decided to take a room in one of the vacant rooms in the facility. He was abrupt and angry with her because she came to work and started vacuuming in the hallways, as her job required her to do in the morning. He proceeded to grab the vacuum cleaner from her hands, took it out of the facility, and threw it in the dumpster. Now mind you, the vacuum cleaner that the facility owned didn't work well, so this employee had taken it upon herself to bring in her own vacuum cleaner in to do her work. So, the vacuum cleaner that was tossed into the dumpster was not the facility's property, it was actually her property, and she didn't dare go out into the dumpster and get her vacuum cleaner back as he said to leave it there. I told her to just rest at ease, I would take care of it for her.

I went to find the owner, and I proceeded to talk with him about the vacuum cleaner that he had thrown away. He was not in the mood to have a conversation with anyone as he had been woken up earlier than he wanted to be, so I thought I would just take care of it. I went out to the dumpster, took the vacuum cleaner out of the dumpster and brought it over to the cleaning lady's car.

As I walked away from the car, I saw the owner standing in the door of the facility. He told me to go and throw that vacuum cleaner back into the dumpster. I shared with him that I was not going to put it back into the dumpster because it was not the facility's property, as it was owned by the employee. Needless to say, he was quite furious with me. He went back into the building slamming the door behind him. A second later, he came back out of the door and told me that I could take the rest of the day off.

I looked up at him and I said, "I can do that, but you would not have anyone in the building to dispense medications to the residents for the first shift." So, with that in mind, he allowed me to come back into the building.

This was the beginning of my journey in paying attention to the staff and to their needs, and in creating ways to make things successful for employees. That particular employee had a tremendous heart, and she wanted to make sure that the facility was clean for the residents. She was kind, she was gentle, and having that type of behavior exhibited against her was just an unfair act.

It even came to a point when he would ask for a resident to receive additional medication because they were bothering him. Which never happened, and it would make him furious to the point where he would leave the building in a rage. It's hard to wrap your mind around the fact that someone like this could actually be in the position to be around this vulnerable population and have such a lack of concern for them, but sad to say, it can happen.

It finally came to a head one day when I went to the office to meet with the Resident Care Director, an RN at the time, and she told me that the owner wanted me gone. He said that I would not follow his directives, and so I knew it was time for me to leave. I prayed that with this RN overseeing the care, that the residents could have a strong lady who would stand up to him as well. I knew she would do her best as she was a great teacher to the care staff and very ethical. I went and said goodbye to all the staff and residents. I told them that I had the gift of knowing each one of them and that I had a new door opening up for me, (which I had no idea what that was), but I had faith that it was going to happen.

The owner found out that I was letting people know I was leaving, and thinking I was conducting it in a way that would cause detrimental disruption, he walked me to the door in his Cheshire cat way in front of the residents. I kept smiling as it was it was during the noontime meal, and I didn't want the residents to be upset. I wanted them to continue the thoughts as to celebrate the next journey that I was about to make. As I left the building, he was standing there with eyes glaring at me, with his back towards the residents and the staff. I raised my hands up in the air as I went to get into my car, and I stated, "God bless you all and keep you safe!" He was red-faced by this point in time. I drove away not knowing what my next chapter was going to be, but having the faith that it was in God's timing.

It was these types of incidents that pushed me further into the desire of becoming an administrator. By the grace of God, these types of owners are not found frequently, at least I hope they're not, and it hasn't been my experience over the 30 years of being in the industry. But having the courage to stand up for what is right, integrity in approach of caring for others, in doing the right thing even when no one is looking, it's that philosophy that has stayed with me throughout my entire career. It was the foundation of every employee I hired. I would hire an employee if they had a kind heart and a desire to do the right thing with an interest in further education all day long, sometimes over people who may have a litany of certificates.

This owner was just a bad seed. He was someone that was in the business for the wrong reason, for profit only. He would have a Cheshire cat approach, and act of being very kind in front of the residents, but behind the scenes, it was a black storm that people were afraid of, which required a sentry of some sort to protect those who could not protect themselves.

There were plenty of angels that helped me along the way during that time, from staff to residents, who encouraged me to continue my education and to follow my passion in caring for others. And as a piece of information for you to know, this man, along with his business partner, ended up being caught for fraudulent acts and using money from the residents inappropriately. You see, they were taking deposits beyond the monthly rent, and they were using these deposits as their own money instead of placing the money into a secure account. It wasn't theirs to use, it was still the residents and should've been used for the last month of rent payment.

I was not aware that this was something that they were doing as I was busy taking care of the residents and helping the staff. I knew the Ombudsman program was an active support for those residents, and they came into the building speaking privately with the residents. The staff had an opportunity to speak with them and any surveyor that came through the door as well. The good Lord knew, and you can't keep things hidden, that are not just. Due process will occur, and those advocates who are there to protect the rights of the residents will prevail, as they did.

This action ended up creating new policy and regulations on how monies are transferred between business owners and residents from that point forward. Again, an experience that created change, and created protection for those who are most vulnerable, our seniors. It fueled the desire in me to continue my journey in being in administrator. All my past experiences as a child were still coming forth. Being aware of my surroundings, taking notice of those who may need protection, and praying for angels to guide me each day.

◈ ASK YOURSELF:

Have you ever stood up for yourself or others that made significant changes in something?

_____

_____

_____

How did your actions change the future?

_____

_____

_____

MY NEXT CHAPTER

Building an LLC and Owning My Own Facility

Who knew that this young lady from a small town in Maine was going to own her own facility? This opportunity came from the very kind gentleman who owned a facility in Falmouth, Maine. This man had a passion for taking great care of our older population and had an exemplary facility. It was an old home that looked like an old Victorian farmhouse. It sat on a hill with pretty grounds all around, and it was a 30-plus bed facility that had the capacity of having state assistance in paying for room and board for the residents; i.e., Medicaid, which now we call MaineCare here in Maine.

The ownership opportunity came to me through two business partners, and we created an limited liability company or LLC, which had bylaws whereby each party had a vote on a business decision, the majority vote, two to one with final decision on a business perspective. The strength of this limited liability was that one of the owners had an accounting background and could manage the books, while myself and the other woman had backgrounds in creating programs and care-related businesses. This LLC was formed in the early 1990's.

It was at this facility where I started having the gift of creating new programs and new ideas with a great team of people. I had this one gal by the name of Lee, who was one of the hardest workers I can remember and was our resident care coordinator. She had the patience of Job and a knack of humor which is helpful in situations when things appeared chaotic, she could calm down the seas. She had that gift of being intuitive, of being able to be still, look at her environment, and make decisions based off the facts that were presented to her, and not be triggered by the chaos around her. She helped me develop a number of programs that we used in the facility, and one was using music therapy in diffusing behaviors and anxiety.

We had this gentleman who would become very, very restless, not aggressive, but just very restless, and my heart would break because I knew how unsettled he was. He had become quite nonverbal, and it would be heart wrenching to watch his wife come every day to hold his hand and watch his eyes as he looked at her knowing he wanted to tell her something but was not able to say it.

One day, she walked up to me as she knew we were doing music therapy. She said to me, "If I brought you a song, would you play it so I could maybe dance with my husband one more time?"

She brought the song to music therapy that afternoon, and we arranged to have it played while she was visiting. Lo and behold, as we played the song, this man lit up. He sat up straight in his chair, then he stood up and he put his hand out and as if to ask his wife to dance.

As they stood in the middle of the room swaying back and forth to the song that they had always shared together, he stopped. He took her hands up next to his chest, as he looked down into the eyes of his beloved wife, he said, "I love you." There wasn't a dry eye in the room, all of us knew that the music unlocked the door to allow him to be able to say those words that he had been trying to say, which were trapped deep inside. What an amazing gift to be able to watch that happen.

You see, this man was a college professor, and he had a routine that he used to do at his work that became an imprint to his being. We focused on this imprint, and we set up my desk with some large books to one side, a mug of coffee, and some papers for him to look at. Each morning, we had him go to my office and have his coffee as he used to do all those years as a professor. He sat up like a light was being turned on and went into his routine from all those years.

This unlocked some conversations that he was able to have after establishing his routine of year's past. He was able to have more words that he shared with his wife than when he first came. It helped unlock those doors in dementia and created some lasting moments with his love, his wife.

◇ ASK YOURSELF:

What song, movie, book, poem or even a scent opens up a door in your memory?

_____

_____

_____

I worked as the resident care director in this facility. One day, while I was sitting at my desk, again, I could hear it as clear as a bell that I had to go to see a person by the name of Bob, a resident on the first floor. It was so strong. It was if someone was whispering in my ear... you need to get up and you need to go see Bob. As I've shared, I've learned not to ignore these types of senses, so I got up from my desk and I walked to his room. As I walked into his room, he looked over at me and raised his hand to me to come towards him. I could see that he was in trouble. As I sat down by his side, he took my hands, and ever so gently, with his eyes looking at me, he passed away right there with my hands holding his. I knew that the good Lord did not want Bob to pass away alone, and He tapped me on the shoulder to go in to be with him as he was transitioning to the other side.

These types of occurrences happened throughout my 30-year career of working in healthcare. I cannot even count the number of times that I was sensing that I needed to go visit someone, or go check on a part of a building to find that there was a need. I have learned to acknowledge and to embrace the active presence, to be able to sense an angel guiding me to be with someone in their hour of need. I have felt so blessed to have these experiences in my life, and they have all taught me beyond measure, a true appreciation in the honor of someone's life. To the "details" in life that make up this world of kindness, appreciation, and growth. To take what one has learned and apply those lessons learned and teach others the quiet gift of recognizing the gift of being a part of someone's life, no matter how small of a moment it may be. To make you strong and determined to see something through to the end, even if it may fail, to take what was learned and apply it forward.

◈ ASK YOURSELF:

Have you ever followed your intuition, and by embracing it, had a profound experience?

_____

_____

_____

When have you seen something difficult through to the end?

_____

_____

_____

LOOKING BENEATH THE SURFACE

Having Lee at the facility allowed me to continue my educational journey and being involved in creating new policies and procedures working with the State of Maine and reimbursement. It also helped us create, with my business partners, a consulting company where we went out and we helped other facilities to be able to work with their staff and help them create programs based on their environment and their needs.

At one point in time, we had nine other facilities that we were assisting. Being able to go in to help people create success in their buildings, in their dreams, and to be able to take care of those beautiful residents was a gift that I will always treasure.

But being part of a limited liability can also come with downfalls. You can be outvoted and you could be put in a position of having to do something that you really didn't want to do. This happened to me in one of the buildings that my business partners decided to go and manage to see if there was a way we could make this building a success. Little did I know of the lessons that I would learn within these walls of this group home.

At first, I didn't see all the potential that was there, but through all the gifts that my mom and dad taught me about discerning and honoring people, and not just looking at the peripheral, I persevered and prayed to see the path that I was to take.

This particular building took care of all men, they were veterans with PTSD and/or a mental health diagnosis. I was in my thirties and I was told that I needed to go and do an assessment of the building to see what we could do to help them. As I drove up the driveway, I could see that the building needed love and care. The grass needed to be mowed, the driveway needed to be swept and paved, and there was a group of guys who did not look very clean sitting out in aluminum chairs in the driveway. I must say, they did not look very welcoming either.

So, I took a deep breath and proceeded to go meet with the person I was told would give me a tour. As I entered the building, my eyes started burning from the smell of urine. I could not believe that I was outvoted to be chosen as the one to go see what I could do to help this facility. I recognized right off that while the staff was kind, they just weren't equipped to see all the things that were available for them. They needed some organizational protocols and procedures, and they really needed a little bit of fun and joy. They were not equipped to care for this population.

I watched their interactions with some of the residents in the building, and I was very impressed with how kind they were. They were doing the best job they could with what they had. I went from room to room and saw the living conditions in this facility, where the kitchen was, where their dining room was, and what they had available for activities for these gentlemen. I smiled, thanked them for their time and told them that we would get back to them and get in touch with their owner about being a consultant and helping them.

As I went out to my car, the gentlemen were glaring at me, wondering who I was. I smiled back and waved, saying have a good day, and got into my car and drove away. Tears started to come to my eyes from seeing the living conditions that these residents were in, and then I realized that now my clothes smelled like urine too. How in the world was I going to help change this living situation?

Needless to say, I was not very happy with the position that my business partners had put me in, but I also knew that God placed me in this position for a reason. I had to have faith and see beyond the first impression that I was faced with in helping these residents. I knew I had to look to my roots for what my father had always told me, and to my mother for giving me the vision of looking for angels walking by. The good Lord knew that I really needed those angels, and I really needed to look at the details of how I was going to be able to help.

One of the first things I needed to address, of course, was the cleanliness of the facility. One of the things I came up with was getting those little round deodorizers that are red that you put in a urinal; so we put them at the bottom of each urinal in the bathrooms. And then, we created a competition for the residents. Mind you, they were all men, and I thought I could tap into this mindset.

This competition was designed so that you had to hit the bull's eye the whole time that you were peeing and not let it go on the floor or walls. Now that may sound kind of funny... but that actually worked. These residents thought it was funny, and they had a competitive nature as most people do. They wanted to prove that they could hit the bull's eye the whole time. Check! The bathrooms stayed cleaner longer!

I then found out that there was community service that needed to be done by some guys I knew, as they had gotten themselves into a little bit of trouble partying and had gotten DUIs. So, I inquired about this community service need and asked for them to be able to come to the building and paint all the bedrooms and the common areas.

I had to create an involvement with the residents and the staff. I researched colors that would create a calming environment and had the residents choose their own colors for their own bedrooms from that palette of colors. The staff was able to choose the colors for the common area through a majority vote. So, the only expense was the cost of the paint and the brushes.

I knew these "volunteers" and their background, so I felt confident in their abilities to navigate the environment, and they ended up having some of the residents sit, watch and talk while they worked. It turned out that they had quite a good time and even came back and visited the residents after the work was completed!

It was amazing to think that you can change the resident's behaviors just by changing the colors on the walls, but it did that and more! The painting project created a little bit of territorial respect and the men wanted to make sure that their rooms were taken care of now that they had fresh paint. It ignited some pride in their environment. In turn, this ended up helping the staff help them in caring for their clothes and picking their stuff up off the floor because now they had a brand-new room that they had chosen the color of and that created a sense of ownership in. Check! A sense of pride in the residents and the staff had been ignited!

The next challenge I had was to figure out how in the world was I going to get these gentlemen to take their showers. They thought there wasn't a need to take showers, and it was very hard for the staff to complete a care plan in making sure their skin integrity was taken care of. We had addressed a lot of the incontinence issue because of the red bull's-eyes program that was initiated in the bathrooms. The facility didn't have the smell of urine that it once had, but now how were we going to be able to get the showers completed?

Almost all of these men were smokers, and those who were not, loved to go out to eat. Some of the residents were private pay, and some were receiving state assistance to pay for their room and board, so we had to consider this in the plan.

People tend to stereotype those that have been labeled with the diagnosis of mental illness. And that stigma was something that I truly felt was placed on my heart to help diminish. These guys were pretty wise about their money and how it was to be spent. I knew I had to try to find a way to make them feel that they were getting a good deal with the money they had to spend to get their cigarettes.

We had a van that we used to transport them back and forth to doctor's appointments. The Activity Director and I, along with the Resident Care Director, who was a very smart young man, came up with a program where on Fridays we would take them to New Hampshire to get their cigarettes. You see, in New Hampshire, they didn't have to pay tax on the cigarettes so they would think they were getting a good deal and would want to go.

The key to getting them into the van was that if they were going be traveling out of state and we are going to be stopping to get something to eat (for those who weren't smokers), that the facility was going to pay for this as an outing event (saving them money). But the only way they were allowed to go was that they would have to take a shower to go on the trip. There would be a sign-up list to join on Fridays to go in this 14-passenger van to New Hampshire to get a good deal on the cigarettes and go out to eat. Check! The residents skin integrity was improving, and they were going on an outing with clean clothes and saving money!

We were on the way to a cleaner, nicer-looking building, the staff was happier because the bad behaviors were being reduced, and the residents were getting better care because they were now having their clothes washed. They had pride in their rooms, and even though they were still smoking, which they were going to do anyway, they felt that they were financially being smart. These gentlemen were starting to have pride, they were starting to smile, and we were able to come up with different opportunities for them to be involved in different tasks to match their capabilities with their past experiences.

I remember one gentleman who came to stay with us who had been homeless for a number of years. He was a very capable young man who was lost and needed someone to believe in him and help him get started again. The facility needed to have a maintenance person, which we had room for in the budget.

I obtained permission from the owner of the building and from my business partners to hire this gentleman as the maintenance person. He had been discharged from the building and was living in an apartment in town. He now had things under better control and had a knowledge that no one else would have of the needs in the building. He was knowledgeable as a handyman, as he had these types of jobs in the past.

Now mind you, this was not something that you would typically see. And the State was questioning whether or not they would allow this to happen. But I reminded them that this gentleman was no longer a resident, and he was a member of the community who had applied for an open position. We interviewed him and decided he was qualified. There was really nothing that the State could do. We had confidence in this young man because he knew the challenges of living in a building with other men, an understanding of mental illness and being able to help people when they were depressed or scared. He would sit with them and just "be" sometimes, not talk, but just be.

One gentleman that had been placed with us was a big man who had psychosis and episodes of intense anger. I got a call from the facility that I needed to go there because this man had picked up a very large scale and thrown it across the room. He was asked to do something, and I believe it was around a medication issue that he was insistent that he was not going to comply to take.

So, I traveled to the facility and met with a couple of staff members to discuss the situation. The gentleman that I had hired as the maintenance person came over to me and he said, "Karen, this is a tough guy. I know this man, and would you allow me to stand beside you because I really don't trust what this man might do. I don't want you to get hurt."

I thought about what this maintenance man was telling me. He was now one of my staff members and thought he knew better than I on how to approach the situation because he had lived in it. He and I walked into the living room where this man was. He had a staff member barricaded on the porch. We proceeded to talk with him about what he needed and how could we help him. At the same time, I knew that we needed to be safe and I had the rescue unit coming because I could not leave the situation in this manner.

With the help of this staff member, who was once a resident, we were able to talk with this man and together, we were able to have the barricaded staff member leave the porch area. We sat with this man until the point that he broke down and started to cry. At that time, I had one of the other CRMA staff members with me, one I knew that he tolerated, bring him his medication to be able to help him, and he took the medication.

If it wasn't for the gentleman that was once a resident and who was now part of the care team and taking care of this gentleman, I'm not sure what the situation would've ended up looking like. Taking the risk and seeing the potential in people is important. Having the faith in the understanding and compassion to be able to help people with mental illness and PTSD is so needed. They need not to be seen as people with a diagnosis of mental illness, but as a person with a name, a person who loves to fish, or has been in war and has seen a part of a world that we cannot even imagine.

Everyone has a need for purpose and to not be categorized as a diagnosis and labeled, but to be seen as a man or a woman who is a member of the community where they live. This is what happened in this community in this little small town in Maine. This facility became a wonderful place for people to work and for people to live. One of the last days that I was there, I was sitting in my office, and I heard a knock on my office door. One of the residents walked in. He was so handsome, with his hair combed and a smile on his face, all dressed up in a suit coat that the activity Director arranged to get from a local Goodwill shop. He said to me, "Karen, would you please come with me for a moment?"

"Of course I will. What's up?" I replied.

He smiled and said, "I would just like you to come with me for a moment. I have something to show you."

I followed him across the driveway to the main building and went down to the dining area. I noticed that the lights were dim, and I said to him, "Oh, you're showing me that I need to do something about the lights in the dining room?"

"No, I just need you to go down to the dining room."

I continued down the stairs to the dining room, and all of a sudden the lights came on in the room. There in the room were all of these men, all dressed up in suit coats, all smiling and proud of how they looked. Men who were men, who had purpose and knew that they were cared for as the person they were, not diagnosed as what they were labeled with. The staff was lined up at the front of the room and there were flowers on the table. They had set up rows of chairs on either side of the room, and had made a path up the middle.

The wonderful man who came to my office and escorted me here asked if I would take his arm as he walked me down to the front of the room. As I started walking towards the front of the room, music started to play and these residents, these wonderful men, started singing to me *"You are My Wild Irish Rose."*

To this day, I cannot speak of this event without crying. Seeing these men who were now people with names within the community that they lived, some of the veterans were going to area high schools and sharing experiences of what they had gone through in war. All this was done by changing the mindset of those who cared for them, of those other people within the community itself, and how they felt about themselves.

Words cannot express the accomplishment and the pride that I had for all of the staff that helped create this moment in time. With the help of the staff and the doctors, we were able to reduce the need for medication by two-thirds. The behaviors were minimized, and we were able to help a number of people to live on their own and be successful in holding down a job.

It was through that training that I had in my deep roots that my dad had taught me on how to look at the details. Like the detail of taking care of those who are veterans, who were over in Europe in World War II. When sirens would go by, or a storm would be approaching, they would become afraid and barricade themselves.

To help address the situation, we had an idea that actually came from the fire chief. He suggested that I get a scanner and have it in my office so that I would know if there was going to be a unit traveling by with their sirens on. We got the scanner, and we were able to communicate to the staff when there was going to be a unit going by with their sirens on, and the staff was able to go to the residents and let them know that this siren that they were going to hear was actually a rescue unit going to help somebody.

Because they trusted me, they were not as afraid, so medications did not need to be dispensed for their anxiety as frequently, and we were better able to work through situations and not be disabled by them. The resident care director would keep track of the weather and the thunderstorms as the residents would sometimes hide behind or under their beds, thinking that it was bombs that were being dropped. By being able to educate them that it was a thunderstorm and that it wasn't bombs that were being dropped, became a positive outcome for the residents in more ways than one.

This building, and this job that I took, changed my outlook in so many ways as it did for others. We did music therapy and we did skits and made sure that we had many times of joy. We even looked into their life stories and protected them as much as possible from things that imitated previous hardships in their lives.

◇ ASK YOURSELF:

When have you taken the time to drill down and see what is below the surface of what seems to be true but isn't?

_____

_____

_____

Have you found yourself in a situation that seemed impossible at first yet you persevered?

_____

_____

_____

If so, how did it change your perspective?

_____

_____

_____

A DIFFICULT LIFE LESSON
ON PAYING ATTENTION

Little did I know, as I was working at this facility helping these gentlemen, that my business partners were having a difficult time with our own facility. I was asked to come to the facility for our quarterly business meeting.

I went to the meeting after work, and we gathered in the office on the top floor of the facility that we owned. As I sat there, I could tell that there was something they needed to tell me but didn't want to say what. I found out that they had not submitted the remittance, which were the billable days for those residents that we were taking care of through Medicaid. I could not understand why someone didn't ask the question, but as my mother would say, it was spilt milk, and there was nothing I could do about it. We just needed to find a way to resolve the situation.

They asked me to call the State to see what we needed to do. The following morning, I went to the facility that we owned, and I proceeded to call the State and speak with the Division of Licensing for Assisted Living Director to see what I needed to do. I felt as though my heart stopped when I heard the words from this woman. She told me that since we had not submitted the remittance over the last four months, three months' worth of those billable days were not going to be paid on because they were beyond the grace period.

My heart stopped, we are a small facility, and I had no idea how we would ever recover from such a deficit in income in taking care of our residents. I was furious at my business partners. They did not speak up earlier and I trusted them without inquiring on a monthly basis about the financials. I felt as though I had let the staff down because I had not checked on them on a monthly basis. They had worked with me the majority of the time when it came to business changes. Now it looked like I was going to have to be the one to face them and to tell them that we were going have to close. We had to go through the process of meeting with the bank and working with the State to place our residents and sell the property or foreclose on the loan.

This business had maintained 95% occupancy, and we were not able to survive this because we were two-thirds occupied by having MaineCare-eligible residents. The MaineCare residents were our Medicaid income, and without this income, we could not remain solvent. All of this had nothing to do with the way the facility took care of the residents. The way that we projected and maintained occupancy was purely on the backs of the ownership of the building and the accounting that took place around it. Two-thirds MaineCare and one-third private pay kept the bills and the staff paid.

I was heartbroken, I was embarrassed, and everything that we had worked for was now in jeopardy. We went through the process of foreclosure, and we placed all the residents in surrounding facilities where I knew that they would receive the best care possible. The prior owner of our building was able to absorb a lot of our staff, so I knew that they had income to take care of their families.

As a Limited Liability Company, we still had our consulting business, but I was hesitant to trust my business partners and didn't know if I wanted to continue in the partnership. It wasn't that my business partners were incapable of doing the job because they were very smart and capable businesspeople. It was the absence of knowing a process/protocol and the lack of submitting a remittance to be paid for MaineCare Medicaid reimbursement that had put the entire business in jeopardy.

Not asking that one question of your business partner or to call the State was something that I could not wrap my head around. The partnership dissolved, and I had to file for bankruptcy. The bank made additional agreements with the other business partners, and because I was the one who had the most knowledge around the operation, it fell on me. Because I didn't know about the four months of remittance not being submitted, it completely turned my life upside down, as it did others. I had been working with people in developing deficiency free buildings, and it was hard for me to hold my head up in the business realm of assisted living.

I remember the day that the gentleman who sold us the building asked me to come visit him. I went to his beautiful office in his brand-new building, and he said something to me that allowed me to pick my head up and continue working within this industry.

He said, "People who know you, know you, Karen. There are a lot of people that want to support you and realize the position that you're in. You've learned a lot in the aspect of working with business partners and things you will never forget. So, hold your head up high, and know that there are a lot of people who believe in you. Go out and continue your consulting work."

Here was my angel that was sent to me to whisper the word in my ear, get up, you can still do this, and so I did. I continued my consultant work, and another journey was opening up for me.

◈ ASK YOURSELF

Who in your life has helped you believe in yourself in a difficult time?

_____

_____

_____

Did it lead you to a better place or unexpected journey?

_____

_____

_____

THE GOOD LORD WORKS
IN MYSTERIOUS WAYS

There is one more thing I'd like to share with you. When it came time to work with the bank, and while we were in the process of going through a foreclosure, I received a call from someone who worked in the licensing department in Augusta. This person proceeded to inform me that it was too bad that I didn't sell my Medicaid beds, as we had already returned them back into the State. They said to me, "They were worth a lot of money."

I was speechless. To think that someone had this knowledge to be able to help us survive the situation and not say anything was beyond my understanding. Again, another lesson learned. We could've operated the facility as a private pay facility if we had sold those Medicaid beds. Lack of knowledge, lack of assistance from someone who knew the circumstances around the operation of our Medicaid revenue to private pay had not informed us, and it had crippled us.

To know there was a key to save the operation of the home of our residents and the employment of our staff was hard to swallow. It was too late, and disbelief of having this known and never saying a word, is something I never forgot. If only I had known to ask the question, maybe it was a reflection of what my business partner went through in not knowing the answer. Whatever it was, I have always taken this as a lesson learned; to always watch out for the other guy, to always seek to help others be successful by sharing my experiences, and to always have the heart to lend a hand up in life.

As my journey continued, there was a day when this same person from the State was back in my life again. Little did I know what was about to happen as the days unfolded before me.

FOR THE SAKE OF THEM ALL

On to my next consulting journey... I remember a time that I had discovered that an owner was rerouting state dollars to his facility in another state. This was one of the toughest positions I have ever found myself in. It isn't an easy road of trustworthy people at times, sad to say. Finding someone to listen and protect the residents at the same time was tough. And even tougher was making sure the staff was paid their wages before the money left the bank!

Through coordinated efforts and deposit availabilities, we managed to get the staff paid week over week. The process was getting more and more difficult as the owner was becoming more demanding in accessing the money before the food was purchased and staff was paid. Finally, one day it all stopped. The staff was making curtains for resident rooms and bringing in food from their own gardens, and the time had come to deliver the residents and staff to the aid of the State.

So, off to Augusta I went with the keys to six buildings in my hands representing over 90 residents and over 100 staff. Into receivership they went, and with the support of the State and an assigned receiver to oversee the operation, the residents and staff were now protected.

The next outcome was hard, the closing of five of the six facilities. It was so sad as these were their homes, and the staff were their family. The staff had to find new jobs and on top of everything, it was found that the owner had taken all of their retirement funds and nothing was left. That particular facility had staff contributing to the fund for over 20 years. My heart broke as there was nothing I could do to help them. We helped through job fairs for those facilities that had closed and job reference letters for those who were able to secure a position elsewhere.

One of the things I remember most was how gracious the residents and families were once they found out how long we had tried to support them. To the best we could, we paid the bills, kept them safe, fed and informed them. We did the same for the staff, and to this day, I have a drawing from one of the employees that was signed by all the staff hanging in my office. It states how much they will miss me as I went onto another position for the company that became the receiver. All those people will hold a very special place in my heart for how brave, enduring and innovative they were to help us get through those times.

A sketch from the staff

Again, the whispers in my ears that my mother told me to listen to, and the attention to detail that my father instilled in me, came to serve those around me. We ran the race as long as we could and then resolved to ask for help to save those in the wake of the storm of injustice. Note to know: the owner who committed all of these offenses to these residents and staff did go to jail. You do not get a pass for being inhumane to the people in the State of Maine!

⬦ ASK YOURSELF:

Have you ever found yourself in a situation where you had to stand up for what is right?

_____

_____

_____

Were you part of the solution?

_____

_____

_____

The "Runner Who Never Ran"

SO A DAY UNFOLDS

Only God Knows the Reasons Why

I shared with you that I had been a consultant working with a man who was caught diverting monies from six assisted living facilities. This man ended up being convicted by the State and went to jail. The good Lord equipped me along with others to deal with this situation and allowed me to use my past experiences to take care of these residents and the staff as well.

The day came when again, we had to close facilities, and this same individual who had informed me about the Medicaid bed dollars that I missed for my own facility was in charge of the receivership process. This person, along with another person from the State, was going with me from facility to facility to see the buildings as we were now going into receivership. Receivership is where the State assigns an official receiver, a management team, to oversee the facility that is now under the control of the State.

As we went into one of these buildings, the residents were sitting around wondering who these people were as I was taking them through the building. We had invited the families to be there as well, to support the residents, so I am sure they didn't feel like it was anything good. It was on that day that we were letting them know that the building was closing. The staff were aware of the circumstances, but the residents had not been told as of yet.

So, as we walked into the room with all the residents sitting around, I proceeded to thank them all for being there, and I said that I wanted to introduce them to someone who had something to share with them. Mind you, I had no idea I was going to say what I said, it just happened within the moment. This person from the State turned to look at me in disbelief that they were now in the position of having to tell these residents that the facility was going to close.

I'm not a revengeful person, and I was as astounded as this person was to the fact that I said it. For some reason, this instance of having to understand the feeling of standing in front of a resident and tell them that the home that they've been living in is no longer going to be available was happening.

We stayed with the residents, the families, and the staff for a while answering questions to what will happen next and how the receivership process works. I had never been involved in a receivership before as well, so I had the same feelings of wondering what I was to do next. We assured them that they would be cared for and that we would find homes for the residents and jobs for the staff as best we could. We wanted to make sure they knew that they were not in this alone.

When we went back out to the van, you can well imagine how angry this person was with me that they had been placed in this situation of having to share the news of the closing with the residents and families. I wasn't sure what I was going to say, so I looked up and I said the truth, "This wasn't preplanned. I'm sorry that you had to experience this, but now you know how a provider feels when telling their residents that their home is closing."

This person just stared at me and (I think) absorbed what it was that I had said, so time stood still. The van became very quiet as we drove off, no one said a word. But for some reason the day aligned to have this experience occur. Believe it or not, after that, this person was very supportive to me and even had me continue working with the receiver. Both of these state representatives became my biggest supporters throughout the receivership.

We never spoke of that day, and we met up in many conferences throughout my career. I only shared events of the day with the receiver, as I still couldn't believe it happened. God works in mysterious ways only known to Him. Whatever His reasoning was, I learned that we never know how and what may transpire in a day, and to have the faith to step forward and support the process.

◈ ASK YOURSELF:

Have you ever had to show compassion to someone who has wronged you?

_____

_____

_____

How did that change your perspective on forgiveness?

_____

_____

_____

There are times in life that we need tools to help us navigate the journey ahead. These tools consist of nuggets of information to help us build those steppingstones as we journey through life.

I have found the writings of John C Maxwell to be most helpful. One of my favorite books is the one that reflects the philosophy that I've embraced throughout my years, it is: *Sometimes you win, Sometimes you ~~lose~~, learn.*

John says in this book, "Humility allows us to make the most out of our mistakes by allowing us to make the most out of our mistakes and failures." He also said, "Novelist Mark Twain was once asked to name the greatest of inventors. His reply: 'Accidents.'"

◈ ASK YOURSELF:

Have you ever reflected upon your own fabric of "living" and what it is all about?

_____

_____

_____

All of these stepping stones, failures, and successes created an amazing life story. Reflecting back to moments of watching my children grow and businesses fail and prosper is all part of what the fabric of "living" is all about. The appreciation of nature that has stayed with me from my childhood transferred over to my management years as we helped residents go fishing and actually taking wheelchairs in the ocean waves to feel the fun again! Each year has imprinted in my soul. From working with great leaders to those who I had to make tough choices about and decisions that changed my view on what a human being is capable of doing.

How did that change your perspective on your life's journey?

_____

_____

_____

THAT SMALL STILL VOICE...

I have always been a person who had a sense of spirit, a sense of direction, or of learned wisdom. There's been something that has always been within me, whether it is a spirit from my grandmother, my mother or my dear, dear second mother, Cam. I have always felt within me a subconscious, of being able to feel and see things around me a little differently than others do.

Throughout my life, I have had multiple occurrences of feeling a sense of presence, an angel is what I call it. That whispering in my ear to go visit someone who needs my assistance. To go look to check on something because as it is broken and dangerous.

Like the time I was sitting at my desk at the facility I was managing in Cape Elizabeth. I was sitting there and heard, as clear as a bell, you need to out to the back deck. I tried to think beyond it, but it was something that I learned not to ignore. So, I stood up and went to the back deck.

◇ ASK YOURSELF:

Do you have a small voice that whispers in your ear and becomes your compass?

_____

_____

_____

There on the deck was the electrical outlet with exposed hot wires laying on the deck. It had somehow been pulled from the outside wall of the building. If a resident had found it, they may have tried to pick it up and since it had live wires, they would have had a shock.

There have been many times in my life that someone would just scratch their head and say, and this was one of them, "How in the world did you know that to be there?" or "How did you know that that resident needed you in that moment, or that the heater in the back hall was leaking water that would have caused major damage to the building?" ... an angel always whispered in my ear, just like my mother always said there was from when I was a child.

Do you listen to it or ignore it?

_____

_____

_____

THE JOB GETS BIGGER

Eyes Wide Open

The next chapter in life took me to a place of working with exemplary people. Those years were days of learning and having creative moments in a changing world of reimbursement. Those whispers in my ears kept coming, and we created a way to record time spent serving the residents to capture the most exact value in time spent. This was shared and trained with many facilities in helping centers to maximize their new reimbursement system. Staff trained staff, and we established a mentor system that created improved employee value. We utilized all the "details" that were within the system and made an advantage to create a positive outcome by maximizing activities for the residents, increasing therapies that were needed to create independence, which in turn improved their quality of life. A win-win for all!

I then received a call from a friend who asked if I would consider coming to work as an executive director for a place in Cape Elizabeth, Maine. This little small-town girl was being interviewed by a national company to manage one of their buildings. Boy was I nervous, and I remember exactly where I was during that first interview with the CEO. I was sitting in a Staples parking lot in South Portland watching the planes go overhead, wondering if I was getting in over my head.

The appreciation in all that the receiver had done for me weighed heavily on me, as I knew how much they took care of me after the incident of the receivership. I never wanted them to think that I was letting them down in any way, but God was opening a door that I was being asked to walk through, and each time He had done that, I kept my head up and listened for that small voice and looked at all the details to weigh my decision.

I had a gift during that interview call, the CEO was from Maine, so we had something in common that I could reference. We went through the call, and he said... "I guess a person from Maine isn't a bad choice for the position," so there was that door opening once more to a new adventure.

I drove up this long winding driveway with ornamental trees all along the way and turned the corner to see a massive gorgeous building. The grounds were landscaped with beautiful flowers and my breath left me... what have I gotten myself into! Lord, please help me!!

Village Crossings

Those next 13 years were some of the most rewarding times I have had in creativity, teamwork, and overall programming. We created a respite program that was one of the first in Maine and took rehab step-down patients that had therapy right in their apartments. We created collaborative programs with area universities where students conducted their fieldwork and pilot studies in our community. We had a nurse that created a model of care that was developed and molded to win Quality awards from the American Healthcare Association and the State of Maine. We had a hospice program, the first in the State in assisted living, that offered dignity and a place of passing that one lady woke to say... "Am I in heaven?" which just brought tears to every person in the room.

This was a journey of whispers and goosebumps in creative moments. Risks and probabilities were stretched to accomplish positive outcomes no one could imagine. We had a nurse who created a Congestive Heart Failure Program that created unimaginable results. We once had a resident in hospice with congestive heart failure that was placed within the program who had gone through all her wishes she needed to do on hospice; her outlook was grim.

Then, something amazing happened! She started getting better, and gaining weight, and was starting to exercise and enjoying activities again, to the point of disbelief of her physician. Her family was in awe not knowing what to do because they had followed her wishes, and divided everything up and now she looked like she was getting ready to be discharged to independence! And independent she became! She moved to a condo by the water, ecstatic to be on her own again and enjoying her family and friends. She became the poster person of our Congestive Hearth Failure Program! When God has a plan, He has a plan!!!

DEVELOPING PROGRAMS THROUGH INGENUITY

What a beautiful journey it was, not to say it didn't have bumps and stumbles along the way. We had some of the most wonderful staff anyone could ask for in the industry. We held staff steady with just a 4% turnover and had a customer service rating of 95-100% year over year. The culture of caring was throughout the community, and this culture served us all—from the vendor to the visitor who walked through our doors.

We did have a few hardships with staff who had lost their way and unbeknownst to us, were stealing from the residents and stealing drugs. With the help of the local police and very sharp eyes from the staff, and dare I say angels, they were caught and prosecuted. We were able to get back most of the belongings that were stolen by a very diligent detective who went to pawn shop after pawn shop searching for the stolen items.

I remember one Christmas Eve when the detective came to the building as he had recovered an item at one of the pawn shops. It was an engagement ring that one of residents received from her husband many years ago in Europe during the war. The lady was 99 years old, and when he showed her the ring, the tears came pouring down and her crying words in Italian thanking the detective radiated the room. Until that day, we had never known the story behind the ring of how she received it, oh, how precious it was. Diligence paid off again, and never giving up on doing what is right was at the core of it all.

I believe the creation of the GRACE model of care opened a door that the good Lord intended to be put to good use. Working with a national healthcare company allowed the financial backing for creativity to grow and prosper. Watching the nurse who created the concept grow as a person and become this amazing leader was astounding. The creativity that she bestowed upon the program flourished in as many as six other communities crossing over to a memory care model as well. She will always be the basis of this program in my mind as the program carries her mother's name, Grace. We all had our jaws drop when we had a roof replaced on the building because the contact paper that covered the entire building had the word, GRACE, as the name of the company. Now tell me that wasn't angel delivered! We were literally sealed in GRACE!

At the same time, we create an occupational therapy program, where, upon admission, we would conduct an interview process in the resident's own home and took notice of their environment and surroundings and of their prized possessions and placement of them so we could replicate it as best as possible. The results were astounding! The admission program reduced behaviors to a previously unimaginable degree. It was creating a world that was kinder and more considerate to those who needed to transition from their home to another world to be safe.

The amount of loss and decline in this transition was found to be immeasurable before the program. After the program was initiated, the loss aspect was reduced, and a transition that normally took up to six weeks now had turned into days, with moments of breakthroughs. Pilot studies were conducted, and staff trainings were developed that truly changed the way of life for those who transitioned from home with memory loss.

The key was having a company that embraced new ideas, new concepts, and allowed us to be able to create a world that was specifically for what was right for the individual, not just what was right for the business. It was intentionally looking at the needs of the person while creating a business model able to fulfill the needs operationally. This functionality was found to sustain a business, and wow, it truly touched the lives of those that resided there as it created a world of purpose. This model became a very profitable business and one that was replicated in six other assisted living facilities from Maine to Ohio.

This way of operation and model of care ended up creating a margin that they were very surprised to see on an operational scale. It was a model of thinking, a model of intentionally looking to what others needed and not focus just on the bottom line, which in turn, took care of the bottom line.

The *My Innerview* consumer and staff rating system, which is the method of how you rate customer service, had found the model to be in the hundredth percentile. It attained national recognition year-over-year as a customer satisfaction model in attaining staff satisfaction, resident satisfaction, and the operation itself became a profitable business model in the industry. It was used across primary populations served, from independent to those who had memory loss.

We taught the staff not to be task minded. By taking the approach of listening to the residents, to their needs, looking within to their world, and to build on their abilities and not just look at their disabilities, or their diagnosis, but to identify them as a person. This model of care ended up creating an occupational therapy healthcare approach in caring for people that was essential. It was a true foundation to identify the needs of the resident and base their care plan upon their "life story" to honor their tapestry of life.

Again, this simple game warden's daughter, who was taught by her parents the simple, but essential ways to honor life was in motion again. A foundation that is made of solid ground is a lasting one and one that is to be taught to your children's children. Always look to the needs of others and your purpose on earth. Whether it is certain type of moss growing on a rock to remedy an ailment or leaving berries on the bush for the mother bear to feed to her cubs, each lesson learned has its purpose in time in our lives.

BACK TO MY ROOTS IN NATURE

Through the years, I have learned that the gift of nature is there for us to use for medicinal purposes. This gift is in our plants and can be transferred into essential oils and also plant-based products to live a healthier life. This continued the appreciation that my father had always installed in me of taking a look around to see what God has given us so that we can help our body naturally.

Through my years as being a manager in assisted living facilities, I would diffuse essential oils to help boost people's immune system, to battle the cold and flu season, and to create a calm environment, especially for those who were diagnosed with memory impairment.

I can remember many times when a resident would walk up to the little diffuser that sat on the table by the front desk, and they would lean over and take the whisper that was coming from the diffuser and have it go across their face. Then, they would smile and walk away. It would melt my heart to see that the residents truly enjoyed the gift of the essential oils that was occurring within the building. We used it as a part of our disinfecting process to cut down on germs, and through the success of this, we were able to attain full flu seasons without episodes.

Over the years of managing healthcare facilities, I can remember only three times of having people with flu symptoms and having to do processes for the building around an outbreak. Mind you, that is in a course of 30 years which is a very astounding accomplishment! This was done through the diligence of my staff in the use of the all-natural products that was kind to the body, but very effective as a disinfectant.

Are you willing or able to take a homeopathic approach to maintain a healthy lifestyle?

_____

_____

_____

◇ ASK YOURSELF:

Do you think you have a fixed mindset or a growth mindset?

_____

_____

_____

How willing and open are you to change?

_____

_____

_____

The "Runner Who Never Ran"

LOOKING FROM THE PERSPECTIVE OF ABILITIES NOT DISABILITIES

We created a program working with the occupational health students from the University of Southern Maine. We established a contract with the universities so the students could do their field work in our facilities. Through this relationship, we created respite programs and also programs that targeted behaviors for those with memory impairment.

In the memory impairment facility, we created a horticulture program so that the residents could go out and get their hands in the dirt and plant vegetables that they would later harvest. Being able to get outdoors into the fresh air and to be able to actually work with the students and harvest the vegetables that they had grown was so fulfilling for the residents, the students, and the staff. This was a targeted way to reduce chemical dependency for outbursts and behaviors, and the outcome was astounding! The reduction in behaviors was seen throughout the program, and it reduced the need to dispense medications to the residents, so it was beautiful to see. The accomplishment resulted in a 50% reduction in medication needed to manage anxiety episodes and behaviors.

For every resident that was admitted, we would do a life story and create a window box outside their room to have their favorite pictures of their life portrayed. A picture story, whether they were a nurse, they loved to go to camp, or any of those things that represented the fabric of the person's life, all of this was displayed within these window boxes. Their life stories were the basis of the care plan that we would use in taking care of the residents. Our conversations and activities would be based on the world that that they knew and loved, and the outcome of looking into their world instead of having them enter a new world that was foreign to them was truly astounding.

If a person was a plumber, we would have a "rummage box" with all these different plumbing materials that they could sit down and safely work with and show the staff what they used to do with the materials. These rummage boxes were made for each and every resident and reflected a piece of their life that was important to the resident themselves. When a resident was having a difficult day, a staff member would take out the rummage box or they would go to the window box outside their room and start a conversation about the resident's life story.

We would also recognize periods in their lives that were of great heartache. We would make sure that we would have a calendar that would identify what those dates were, and we would honor that point in time. We would make sure that we had something special for that person on that day. It was amazing to have a memory impaired person who may not be able to feed themselves any longer, but who would still have that life memory that was living deep down inside them.

Never underestimate the thoughts within a person diagnosed with dementia. They may not be able to express what is in their mind, but it is truly present. Having these dates honored and held dear made all the difference in their lives. It was an imprint of their life that needed to be honored. Again, the gift of my childhood came through in caring for those around us through gardening, essential oils to calm the soul, and to honor one's life as the gift that it is.

The simple task of being present and listening to all that is being said around you with verbal and nonverbal intuitiveness is one thing I learned being the daughter of a game warden. My father was one who expressed very little in words. He took the time to assess his surroundings. He would look at the land, he would look at the trees, he would look at the weather, and he would look to see who or what had been in that area. He pulled all the information together before he came to a conclusion.

He also embraced the natural aspects of nature, such as the story of the deer that the logger reported that only had three legs. He went to see if there was something that needed to be done for the deer and to make sure that it had food to eat. When he arrived, as you have read within his notes, he noticed that the deer was surviving very well. He had healed and was at full weight, so there really wasn't anything that my father needed to do at that time as a game warden. The deer had learned to adapt to its abilities.

That is one thing my father has taught me through the years, to look at abilities and not just focus on disabilities. Focusing on abilities is very much like what an occupational therapist would do during their assessment of a resident. We used this technique time over time which created purpose in the lives of our residents, to shine on the gifts that one still possess, and to find ways for it to be embraced.

◈ ASK YOURSELF:

Are you aware of non-verbal cues in conversations?

_____

_____

_____

Can you identify the ways in which you communicate non-verbally?

_____

_____

_____

What have you had to change or do to adapt to your own abilities?

_____

_____

_____

Respite Program for Assisted Living

OUT OF THE BOX
THINKING

I have always had a passion for those who were occupational therapists because their job was around hope and maintaining purpose. In the facility that I managed, we created one of the first respite programs in assisted living in the State of Maine. We were helping people to go home; it was called a *"A Maine Bridge to Home."*

We would set up an apartment with all the adaptive needs for respite care. In this studio apartment, a person would be discharged from the nursing home after having an acute care stay, and they would transfer to a home-like environment to safely learn how to be able to maneuver things in their home.

The occupational therapist, with permission from the client, would go to their home and would assess how the room was set up, how their bedroom was set up, how their bathroom was set up, and try to replicate that within the respite room they would be transferred to. They would bring some personal items that the family member had approved, such as their favorite quilt or their favorite books and put them by their bedside. It would be staged to look like they were in their own home. We even would make sure they had some of their family pictures set up strategically to encourage them and help them feel like they were one step closer to being home.

Most of these admissions lasted around two weeks, and then we had the gift of being able to celebrate the discharge to safely go home. The last piece of the program was that they went home with the occupational therapist to continue their care in their own environment.

This program became so popular that we would keep at least three respite rooms available for respite need discharges from the area's nursing homes. I would say that these rooms were occupied at least 90% of the time. Again, the game warden's daughter helping the person to adapt to their environment so that they could safely reside in their own home was no different than the deer that my father helped that time so long ago. I'm sure he went back and checked on the deer from time to time, and the loggers would've been able to communicate whether or not they saw the deer or not. It always me made me proud to be able to say that I was walking in my father's footsteps of allowing people to adapt to their environment and enjoy life in their own habitat.

⬦ ASK YOURSELF:

What's an example in your life where you or someone you know did something out of the box?

_____

_____

_____

What does taking the risk of being first at something mean to you?

_____

_____

_____

SOMETIMES YOU WIN, SOMETIMES YOU ~~LOSE~~ LEARN

One book I like to reference that shadows what I have experienced in life is John C. Maxwell's, *Sometimes You Win - Sometimes You ~~Lose~~ Learn*.

In Chapter 3, he references the heavyweight boxer name Evander Holyfield. He said, "Everyone has a plan until they are hit." He emphasizes that the stress of a difficult situation can make you forget your plan. This was true in the situation of our company's facility where my business partner did not submit the remittance for payment. He didn't process them and then got caught in the web of... Now what do I do??!! He hid and didn't say a word until it was too late. He didn't make the adjustment, which was exactly what Maxwell references in his book. He said, "While it is true that acceptance of a problem does not conquer it," but facing it, and making the proper adjustments can improve your odds!

We were hit, as with the boxer reference, and if we had not gone through the experience, then I would not have been equipped to make the adjustments in the case of the owner that was stealing the resident's money and the staff's 401K. I would have not pushed myself to find adjustments that could keep the staff paid and the food purchased. All these lessons learned came from episodes in my life that gave me an opportunity to learn.

Throughout my entire career, I have taught people how to think out of the box. To not look at limitations as obstacles, but as building blocks of adjustments that help you attain the goal that you're trying to achieve. No one thought we could create a Congestive Heart Failure Program in assisted living with just the expense of a $26 scale, but that was the tool it required along with Registered Nurses who could change the prescription based off the resident's weight. But that is all we needed.

This ingenuity was derived from a very talented LPN who happened to be my Director of Nursing. She was the definition of ingenuity. She came up with protocols that kept the facility almost free of having those superbugs, the norovirus and the flu. I can count on one hand how many incidents we had of these viruses in 13 years. We had a team of staff who met and brought together protocols and procedures, from how many times the contact points were wiped down a day, to the changing of your shoes when you went home so you didn't bring anything home to your family. We diffused essential oils that assist in building up your immune system and universal precautions that were taught from the time you were hired along with monthly training based off the admissions we may have had or a new medications that was being dispensed.

My job as the administrator was to "sell" the idea to the powers to be and implement the programs during budget season. I also had to find the dollars to support the program. I was the one who needed to forecast those adjustments by researching the need for care in the community and find a way to service it.

The world is very different today, as I did not have the sad and difficult situation of facing Covid in a facility. But we dealt with the "adjustments" that is, the actions, that take place and the change in mindset that needs to occur. Each administrator today has a huge job in maintaining all the regulations and all the

safety requirements to keep everyone safe. It is that same ingenuity that people have had to do to face this virus, and God bless
them all for making adjustments and finding the dollars to keep
people safe.

```
The real warriors in this world
are the ones that see the
details of another's soul.
They see the transparency behind
walls people put up.
They stand on the battlefield of
life and expose their heart's
transparency, so other's can finish
the day with hope.
They are the sensitive souls
that understand that before
they could be a light they first
had to feel the burn.
-Shannon L. Alder
```

This writing by Shannon L. Alder is that same reflection of
learning my father and mother instilled in me... by living life and
taking that risk that pushes the edge. To be sensitive to rules and
boundaries and to always find ways to bring hope to a difficult
situation. Standing on the facts and the truth will never fail you;
they are not emotional, but simply pieces of the tapestry that
may look all jumbled from behind, but when you turn it around,
you see the end result. It is the plain truth of the event(s).

These approaches were what I would use as an expert witness,
when I was reviewing cases for attorneys. Operational decisions are led by regulations and Standard Operating Procedures
(SOPs) of the license you held as a business. The SOPs were the
company's application of how things were done and the responsibility of the administrator to adhere to them. These are the

threads that create the pathway that we use in caring for people. It would always surprise the opposing attorney that I did not have a litany of degrees, but that I was there in this position of being an expert witness purely on the face of "experience" and stating the facts of knowing the regulations and how the process of operating a facility under these guidelines.

I've always thought that these are the trails in life, like the ones my father showed me along the shoreline at camp. These trails have now become trials in life. Trials not where you were being charged or judged by but trials where you are creating rules like due process, such as rules of law/lessons that help you to navigate a path in life that is being placed before you to accomplish.

◈ ASK YOURSELF:

When did what you thought would be the worst thing that could happen turn out to be the best thing that could happen?

_____

_____

_____

FINDING THE KEYS

I carried that same philosophy through my entire career as an administrator of assisted living facilities. I would use these care philosophies even when I would go visit my mom, who had sadly been diagnosed with Alzheimer's herself. It was so difficult to watch her struggle, but I used the keys that have been taught to me by my mom and my dad through the years, and I focused on the abilities that she still had, her keys that she still possessed, so I could open doors and be able to have her light shine through once more.

I remember the time when she had decided she didn't want to eat anymore. She had become nonverbal and didn't have any interest in life anymore, her spark seemed to have disappeared. I knew I needed to find her "keys" so I could help her feel the love that was around her, her family and her memories that she still had locked inside.

At that time, I was working in the Sanford area, and I remember driving home from work when I had this desire, this need that I had to stop at the grocery store. I felt the need to go to the meat market and see if they had fresh lobster meat. One of my mother's keys was her love of lobster. She would love her lobster rolls about as much as she loved her ocean. When we would go to the ocean in the Kennebunk area where her sister lived, she would take a little dixie cup, and walk out into the water and dip the cup into the water and she would actually drink it.

I would look at her and say, "Mom, that's very salty, why do you drink the salty water?"

She would say, "I just love the smell of the ocean, and I want to take a little bit back with me, so I'm going to take a sip."

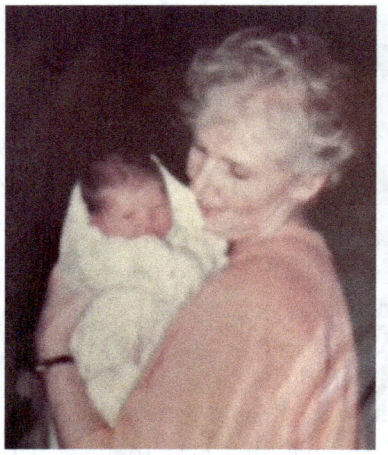 

Mom with Brandy   *Mom's Birthday*

So, I took this memory key, and I decided that maybe if I bought her some fresh lobster meat it would trigger that memory of her loving the ocean and maybe that smell of the lobster would unlock that trigger and she would eat it. So, I walked to the back of the store, and there was a gentleman standing behind the meat market counter, so I asked him, "Do you have any fresh lobster meat, sir?"

"Actually, we do," he said. "It just came in today."

"I'd like a little container of your freshest lobster," I said. "I'm bringing it to my mom as she has stopped eating, and I'm praying that it would help trigger a memory of how much she loves lobster, and start eating again." I said this with tears in my eyes. The gentleman looked at me, turned, grabbed a small container and went out back to get the fresh lobster. He went over to weigh the container as they always do, and he took a pen, wrote on it and handed it to me.

"I'll pray too that your mom eats the lobster and starts eating again, God be with you," he said with tears in his eyes as well.

I said thank you to this very kind man and started walking back to the cashier to cash out the lobster. I looked down at the label that he had put on the little dish of lobster. The price was one dollar, and he signed it. This kind gentleman passed this onto me to give it to my mom as a gift, a gift of hope that it would open the key of wanting to eat again.

I drove to the nursing home where my mom was residing at the time. I sat with her at a little table by ourselves, and I opened up the lobster container.

"Mom, I have something here for you," I said.

She wasn't looking up at the time, and I lifted it up to her nose so that she could smell it. She pulled her head back at first, as if to ask me to take it away from her. All of a sudden she stopped and she looked at me, and then she looked down at the fork that I had put a little piece of lobster on, and she opened her mouth. I was able to put it in her mouth and she started chewing. I sat there with tears in my eyes knowing deep inside this was unlocking a memory of how much she loved her lobster.

She ate the lobster, only a few pieces, but she did eat, and that was that gift of hope, that "key" which unlocked her desire to eat again. Being at that level of need in her journey through having Alzheimer's, it was one of those "windows" that we were able to unlock from time to time, which we all treasured. We all longed to see her beautiful smile and that twinkle she had in her beautiful hazel eyes. Seeing it that day, for that moment in time, it was a gift I will always treasure. I will also never forget that man who helped me unlock this gift, and his prayer that he said that day.

My mother was a person who loved life and all that could come from it. She loved to fish, she loved to go to camp, she loved to hunt, she enjoyed the woods, she loved the smell of flowers, and she had such a gift in gardening. People would stop by just to see her irises and peonies.

There were so many talents that my mom would embrace, and I had the gift of watching her in my younger years growing up in our small town. People would say, "Your mom, Jean, she's the kindest woman I know." And that she was... I keep a picture of her by my coffeemaker with her beautiful smile and that twinkle in her eye.

My morning coffee with Mom

She was a striking redheaded beauty with a spark for life, and the hardest worker I have ever met. She would be up before dawn and one would wake to the smell of coffee and muffins when you came down the stairs. She had a voice of a songbird and would tell us stories of how she once sang at the Merrill Auditorium when she was a young girl. Oh, how I loved listening to her sing. We would sing while doing dishes after a meal and in the car as we drove to get groceries. She loved her convertibles and dad made sure she always had a beauty. As kids, we would ride in the backseat on a summer day with the wind swirling our hair all around while kneeling turned around backwards watching the road behind us. The radio would be playing, and mom and a friend would be in the front while the kids played in the back.

On summer days on the weekends, Mom and Dad would take us somewhere for a picnic, a much quieter ride with dad along, of course, but what fun we had in those convertibles. They would shine so much that you would see your reflection in them as you walked by. Dad always had shiny vehicles, a washed tar driveway, and freshly mowed grass. We had competitions in the neighborhood for who could grow the biggest cauliflower or cabbage and who had the first cucumber.

These are all part of my memories growing up in a small town. They showed me gift of loving nature and all that it can share with you. Mom and dad loved to fish, this is a picture of her and dad in their younger years enjoying a winter's day of ice fishing. You can be sure they had full bellies that night from the fish they caught that day.

Dad and Mom Ice Fishing

◇ REFLECT:

Share some memories and reflections here:

_____

_____

_____

_____

_____

_____

_____

_____

_____

_____

_____

_____

PLANTING SEEDS

Those traits served me well through my years of management as the grounds of the facility I managed were always groomed, and the buildings were always clean. The joys of gardening, for those who desired it, was available so that people could continue their "abilities" in the joy of planting seeds and watching them grow. They would harvest the vegetables and bring them to the kitchen so they could be cooked and brought to the dinner table to enjoy with their friends.

Village Crossings Dining Room

I remember one time I was on the second floor of one of the buildings that I was managing, making up the bed and helping the room get ready for a respite stay. It was a gorgeous summer day, and I stopped to look outside through the window to gaze at the landscape, and there on the lawn, I could see one of our residents, she was laying on the ground. I immediately called down to the front desk, thinking that someone had fallen, and wanted to make sure someone was out there to help them. Much to my surprise, when we went out there to try to assist this woman lying on the ground, she was actually purposely down there so that she could plant her seeds one by one in her little flower garden.

You see this woman had Parkinson's. And it was very difficult for her to be able to walk, and to be able to bend over and do those types of tasks. The occupational therapist had helped her down to the ground so that she could take her seeds and plant them one by one. She even had a little watering can there so that she could water her seeds as well... and so it was... it wasn't an accident with someone falling, it was the gift of being able to do the things that one can still do.

Never underestimate the human heart. The desire she had of gardening had her persevere through her difficulties. No longer was she being limited by having Parkinson's as she was able to enjoy her gardens once more. Again, those treasures and those appreciations of the simple pleasures of life that I enjoyed while growing up in a small town in the western mountains of Maine were ever so present in my life again.

Oh how bright was the light of hope in a world where people are labeled by their diagnosis and set limitations. Watching that all get peeled away to where one could enjoy the pleasure of planting her seeds, one by one and harvesting the herbs to enjoy with her friends was priceless. Never underestimate the human heart and the will to experience joy.

We would call them the keys to one's life. We would always complete a document around their life story so that we knew the things that were important to them, important dates. important memories, things to be able to keep alive so they could keep that memory alive and be with them to celebrate and to mourn, if needed.

We would help people who were wheelchair-bound and take them down to the beach and roll them out into the waves so that the waves could splash against their legs. They could smell the ocean and feel the water upon their legs. They would laugh and smile and talk for hours about that experience to their families and the other staff and residents. It truly was amazing to be able to see how such a simple act would make such a difference in somebody's life.

We would take the men fishing so that they could have that chance again to get that "big one" on the hook. People would drive by this one fishing hole and they would slow right down and look at this gentleman sitting on the seat of his walker with a fishing pole extended over the edge of the bank. Sometimes they didn't notice one of our staff members standing beside him, and they would stop to see if he was okay. They would laugh as they would talk about the day and say, "I wonder what the person is thinking about seeing me out there fishing, sitting on this walker."

Those life stories that we gathered upon admission were the keys to being able to help the person to still have purpose and joy in life. Intentionally looking to the needs of others was a continuance of what my dad had shared with me growing up by watching to see what the deer may need to survive in the woods. Here it was again, a life of reflecting upon a three-legged deer, but really, it is just that simple. Just because one may not be whole, does not mean that their dreams and their experiences have faded away. Creating a way to capture their capabilities to participate in life with the abilities they still possessed was key. The imprint of my childhood and all the tools in my toolbox that my parents had instilled in me were being continued in my work.

A COUPLE OF STORIES THAT I WILL ALWAYS REMEMBER

Making a Difference Once Person at a Time

This is a story of a program that a lovely nurse started as part of her certification in leadership. The program is based on a philosophy of caring and making a difference in someone's life. This is how it goes...

There once was a little boy who was playing on the edge of the water at the ocean. As he walked down the beach to play in the waves, he noticed hundreds and hundreds of starfish lying in the sand next to the water. He looked up and down the beach, took a deep breath, leaned over and started picking up the starfish. One by one, he tossed them back into the ocean so that they could live.

As he was tossing the starfish back into the ocean, an older gentleman came walking down the beach. He watched in amazement as to what the young boy was doing. He stopped and said to him, "Why are you throwing the starfish back into the ocean? You will never be able to get them all put back in the water. What difference can you make?" The little boy reached down and picked up a starfish. He held it in his hand and then he tossed it out into the water. He turned around with a smile on his face, looked up at the man and said, "It made a difference to that one!"

This was the philosophy of the care model she created. The philosophy was of looking at one person at a time, to make a difference in their life, and to help them live a more full and purposeful life. The goal was to create a life embraced with dignity and respect, with a focus on their mind, body and soul. The logo she created included an image of a starfish.

Like the little boy who helped the starfish back into the ocean, she named each one the five arms of the starfish and gave it the word GRACE after her mother. It stood for the Gift of Renewal through Activities Caring and Exercise. This beautiful young nurse started a program that changed many people's lives by replicating the philosophy one person at a time. How blessed I was to be a part of this program and to see it flourish and help people live again.

Hiding in Plain Sight

It has been interesting, over the years, how this phrase has been applied to programs that we've created. Like the situation at that all male facility, where the veterans were being labeled based on their diagnosis instead of their kindness and their talents, once unveiled. Hidden behind their rough persona were gentlemen waiting to come out. They needed someone to look beyond first impressions and the diagnosis and stereotype that is customarily seen. It took time to get to know them and to respect them as the men they were and to unpeel the self-inflicted visions that seemed to be the norm.

Little did I know at the time, that I was applying an occupational therapy approach to care. The little boy's story with the starfish applied once more. This approach intentionally looked at the abilities that they still had instead of labeling them through their disabilities based on expected results from a pre-judging world.

This held true in another experience we had while working with first-year grad students on their way to becoming physicians. We created student field working contracts with area universities so students could come to the facility and work with their professor and our residents in field learning. One of the teaching lessons was this story.

In the building that was in an independent living community, we had some residents who had initial stages of memory loss.

The students would go in groups of two or three to interview the resident in his or her apartment. These residents had offered to be a part of the program as they found it interesting to be helpful to these students who were studying to be doctors.

After the students interviewed the resident, they would come back to a room where either myself, a nurse, or the admissions director would be there with the professor. The students would tell us the story of what they found once they interviewed the resident. It was always very interesting to see the outcome. A resident who had been diagnosed with an initial stage of dementia in our building had an occupational therapy program where we would create a world of success for them in their own apartment. By creating this world, it allowed the resident to retain their life memories by placing different prompts throughout the room. This helped them navigate each day successfully.

It was interesting, as the students came back to report on their findings from their interview and they would say how cognitive and intact the resident was. They would have named their grandchildren and places that they lived along with some stories from years ago. After they gave us their report, the professor and the facility representative would share with the students the story behind the story. The students didn't notice that beside the picture of their grandchildren was the name of each of the people portrayed. Underneath some photographs of their home, where they either grew up or where they raised their family was the name of where this was and the date when they lived there. All of this information was hiding in plain sight, and it helped the resident navigate each day. This helped them to not become frustrated because of the memory loss they were experiencing.

This was a program that was set up through occupational therapy to create success by intentionally looking at their life story and make it a living reality within their environment. The students would be in amazement that they didn't pick up on the prompts and thought how respectful it was since it maintained the dignity of the resident. This program and its structure was used by other area universities in our facilities for those who were on their way to becoming physicians, occupational therapists, physical therapists, and other disciplines as well. This program was a win-win for all involved as it was a living program that we hoped would stay with those students throughout their career.

Freedom of Expression

Believe it or not, we actually created a forum whereby residents could choreograph their own skits with the staff and the residents families. They would put on plays and talent shows for all to enjoy. The residents titled this group of people...The Village Players.

One play that they put together was absolutely hilarious. The staff and the residents did a skit that was named, "Is our Executive Director Dead?" Now mind you, I was the Executive Director. So, they had a story where on one side of the theater-like area that they created was a desk with a person playing the Executive Director, who was played by a staff member. She wore a business jacket and was lying forward on her desk while sitting on her chair with her face planted on her desk.

They had created the skit to have multiple people go in and out of the office. As they did, they would each look to see if the Executive Director had moved. She looked as though she had died in her plate of food. The staff and the residents portrayed different managers that were in the building as they would walk to the door to see if the Executive Director was really dead.

The script was having them in a flutter not knowing what to do. So finally, they asked the person who was portraying the Admissions Director to go in and try to see if they could hopefully wake up the Executive Director or check if she (I) had really died. The script had everybody rolling in the room with laughter. To tell you the truth, I was laughing so hard I was crying.

The Admissions Director went in to see what was going on, and he went over to touch the shoulder of the Executive Director. She popped her head up in a surprised expression with ketchup all over the side of her face. The staff member who was portraying me in the skit was hilarious. She tried to cover up the fact that she had ketchup all over her face and act like nothing whatsoever had happened. The Admissions Director tried to explain that everybody thought that she had died. She responded, "I was only trying to eat my hamburger, and I fell asleep mid-bite!" I will always remember that day, and I can still hear the laughter as it radiated in the room.

The lady who was creator of *The Village Players* was someone who had been diagnosed with Lyme disease and was confined to a wheelchair. She had difficulty speaking, but with the help of occupational therapy, the staff, and devices, she was able to unlock all those lovely stories that were within her mind and continue the playwriting that she had done most of her life.

◇ ASK YOURSELF:

What are some of the stories of your life that you always remember and love to share?

_____

_____

_____

Why do those stories make you smile?

_____

_____

_____

MAKING THE IMPOSSIBLE POSSIBLE

I remember when we created the first hospice program in assisted living. A lot of heads were tipped to the side in wonderment of how this could be done. We had the support of the company that we worked for, a national company named Kindred Healthcare, as they had the confidence in us that we would review the regulations for both the hospice world and the assisted living world to make sure we would be in compliance. So this we did. Honoring the safety nets created by both of these worlds through their regulations so one could receive hospice services in an assisted living setting.

We created it first in a memory care facility as we had a resident who needed hospice services and wanted to stay at the facility. The client's family could choose from a number of hospice service agencies that were in the area to allow the act of choice of service. We would develop business agreements with these hospice agencies as to educate them on how we would comply with assisted-living regulations, and what was available for staffing to be able to support the hospice service. When families knew that they would be able to have their loved ones stay in their room through the end of their life, it was comforting to people.

We created specific hospice training for our staff and made sure that those who were assigned had a desire to serve in this way and be a support through the end of life. It is difficult to lose those residents who you have taken care of day after day, as they become very close and create friendships. We made sure they had support from the hospice agencies and our own management to be equipped to support the transition through the end of life. The program was very well received, and the families were so grateful to have their loved one reside in their own room with the staff and support of familiar faces.

Village Crossings Patio

We then created those same hospice services in an independent care facility that we managed in Cape Elizabeth. This was an apartment setting of one bedroom, two bedroom, and studio apartment living with medical services available by RNs, LPNs, CNAs, CRMAs and PCAs. This facility even had its own restaurant where they could receive their meals, delivered to their apartment like room service in a hotel or they could enjoy their meals in the dining room.

We had already established the respite program in this building, and now we were adding hospice services for our residents as well. It allowed the residents to be able to stay in their home-like environment through their journey to the end of life. One of the hospice agencies had come to me with a dream that she had of always wanting to have a hospice room set up in a beautiful studio apartment like we had in this building.

We created this contract where they paid a daily rate to reserve this room, and when they had someone who was in need in the community and they didn't have a place suitable for the services, they would transfer this client over to our building so that they could have their hospice services in this beautiful room. Mind you, this was a beautiful facility that was nestled within the community of this coastal town of Cape Elizabeth. It had all the coastal beauty surrounding it within its grounds and amenities.

One day, we had an admission in this program of a lady in her 30s. She was homeless and was dying, and in need of these services through hospice. This hospice agency had a dream that the services of hospice didn't rely on the amount of money you had to receive hospice care. They felt that everyone deserves the right to be able to have this type of care in a beautiful setting such as this. They arranged for her to be delivered to the building in a rescue unit and they transferred her up into the room that was on the second floor overlooking the beautiful grounds of the facility.

A Respite Studio

The room was purposely designed to give comfort with specific artistry on the wall and color tones to be able to offer peace to one as they transferred through this end stage of life. The staff had been trained by hospice services on what to do and proceeded to take care of this beautiful woman who was just brought into this facility with barely a clean shirt on her back. They cleaned her up and placed her in this beautiful gown that we had for this hospice room.

I happened to come into the room after they had helped this young lady, and I was there when she fully opened her eyes to look around. Now mind you, this lady had been living on the streets and had been struggling most of her life. She had been in and out of consciousness since she arrived.

She looked up at one of our nurses who was sitting beside her bed holding her hand, and she said to her, "Ma'am, is this heaven?" My heart stopped, and there wasn't a dry eye in the room.

The nurse looked into her eyes and said, "No, my dear, you're in Cape Elizabeth. You are in our room that we call, '*A Walk in Rose's Garden.*'"

The young lady looked around and said, "It sure looks like heaven to me." And within an hour, she passed. The gift of being able to give that one moment in time to this beautiful soul is something that I will treasure forever.

There were a number of times and experiences when we were able to do things such as this for people who stayed at "*A Walk in Rose's Garden.*" We had a flower garden out back where we did a rock of remembrance for each person who came through Rose's Garden. Families would come visit the garden and take moments of reflection and visit with the staff.

A few months after starting this program, the State of Maine changed the hospice regulations so that this particular hospice-paid program by the agency was no longer able to function as a hospice service. It was so sad to have to cease the program that was the dream of this hospice agency owner but we kept our hospice program operating for those who transitioned through end of life as our residents. We knew that every person that came through Rose's Garden was there for a reason, and we treasured every moment we had through that journey.

With these amenities and programs, we became one of nine assisted living communities to have earned a Silver Award–Achievement in Quality Awards from the American Health Care Association/National Center for Assisted Living in 2016. It's the highest number of Silver Awards that have been given to assisted living communities since the program's inception in 1996. In 2022 the American Health Care Association awarded the Silver Award of excellence to 46 recipients with 3 of them awarded to assisted living communities. It is nice to know that this program is still awarding these quality awards to these hard-working long term care communities.

The award is the second of three progressive distinctions possible through the AHCA/NCAL National Quality Award Program, which is based on the Baldridge Performance Excellence Program. At the silver level, members develop and demonstrate effective approaches that help improve performance and healthcare outcomes. This was a tremendous accomplishment for all those who worked together as an amazing team in this community. We became the first in the State to have a hospice program, a respite program to help people go home after a rehab stay, and we created a congestive heart failure program that literally changed lives. What an honor it was to be a part of this journey.

I believe that all this ingenuity and the ability to see the needs of others was a true gift from my father and my mother. The gift to listen, watch and intentionally look at the needs of others and place them first instead of looking at just the business model that needed to be done to hit the bottom line was beyond important. We would say that we would turn the Christmas tree upside down, fill the tree up with all the needs that people said needed to be done, and it would drip out at the bottom, and there it would be.

A group of like-minded people with the purpose and intent to make a change in life and to create a better life for those who need it most, our older population. It was with these like-minded people that we built all of these programs, with the backing of a company with an open mind and the confidence of being able to trust that we were meeting the needs of others. Through this, we would create a business model like no other.

> **ONE DAY** you will realize that after all the battles you've fought, all the storms that you've survived and every mountain that you've climbed, you've always had the strength to make it through life's journey.
>
> *Roger Lee*

From the time I was little I was drawn to hear people's life stories. I would go visit an elderly gentleman that I called grandpa who lived in a house next to ours. I would go and sit and listen to the stories that he would tell me of all the days of yesteryear and be amazed by everything that I would hear.

This compassion was instilled in me from the time that I was little, this compassion to honor mind, body, and soul, to make sure that you help those who need it most, to take the time and listen and honor their lives. This was the gift from my parents that I so treasure. The art of following a rule and to make it your friend instead of your foe.

This was the art of embracing regulations and using them as possibilities instead of restrictions. I have always been a rule follower, to a fault. Embracing it to be able to look at the possibilities instead of focusing on the restrictions is what I have done throughout my years in management. It is like turning the Christmas tree over and letting the programs drip out that was constructed by the needs of others. Not what I thought their world looked like, but one that embraced the stories of their lives, their joys, their accomplishments, goals and profession. It was always their steppingstones, and their trailways of life that we honored in keeping their memories alive.

How have you turned obstacles into opportunities for growth?

_____

_____

_____

What obstacle are you facing now that could become an opportunity with some creative thinking?

_____

_____

_____

RETIREMENT JOURNEY

I retired from administration and my employment from the building that brought so many blessings. I say building, as the management had changed ownership, and we did not envision the programs and staffing levels in the same light. So, I retired from the building, and from all the beautiful people who worked and lived within its walls.

I found myself still hearing that small voice that I was supposed to continue my walk in helping those in need. As if an answer to that, an opportunity came along to join a non-profit called *Sebago Lakes Region Fuller Center for Housing.* This opportunity allowed me to continue to assist seniors, as their mission was to help older people stay safely in their homes and have a decent roof over their heads. "Helping to build a better world, one house at a time."

As our chapter president and friend states,

> *"We are a faith driven and Christ-centered organization that promotes collaborative and innovative partnerships in an unrelenting quest to provide adequate shelter for all people worldwide. The Fuller Center was founded by Millard Fuller, the same visionary who started Habitat for Humanity."*

The *Fuller Center for Housing* is an international organization that is built on covenant partners. These covenant partners consist of over 90 chapters throughout the United States and beyond. In fact, we are the only chapter in New England. We currently have six churches and one college as our supporting founders to our local chapter here in Maine. Our demographic outreach consists of the Windham, Standish, and Raymond areas in southern Maine. This is encompassed in the area around Sebago Lake, hence its name, *Sebago Lake's Region Fuller Center for Housing* https://sebagofullerhousing.org for more information.

So, check! I'm still involved in helping people stay safely in their homes and creating programs and connections with local universities and businesses. It was as if the other end of my program that we created years ago, A *Maine Bridge to Home*, came to life again!!

So here again, we created partnerships with a local university where students would complete their level one fieldwork in the homes of our clients after we repaired their steps, maybe their windows, or their walkways.

The way the *Fuller Center* is set up is that a group of people get together as volunteers to do the work and the labor to complete a project at no cost. If there are materials that are needed, we use a program called the *Greater Blessings Program* where the client pays us back or, as we put it, pays it forward to help others with the purchase of their materials with a zero interest rate applied.

After we've assisted one of our clients, there were times I would see that there was great need for a continued service to be done in the home. They needed help with their balance or with their nutrition, which was limited due to their inability to stand and cook their food. So, I would reach out to the university and connect them with the students, and they would go out with a field professor and assist the person with their needs in their home as a level one fieldwork project.

We call the program at our local Fuller chapter, *"Generations helping Generations."* The students call themselves, *"Fuller's Helping Hands."* Check! I'm back helping students achieve their degree and working with a dear professor that I have worked with for many years in the buildings that I managed.

This relationship has changed lives in more ways than anyone can count. It has helped people graduate to achieve their degrees in occupational therapy. It has helped people to be able to go home and have the support that they need to stay safely at home.

I am always in awe to how the good Lord orchestrates the tapestry in life. Nothing is ever an accident, and I am blessed to a part of the plan. We are now working on a project where the students learn how to write grants for their capstone in their doctorate program in Occupational Therapy. Instead of mock grants, they will actually assist in helping a community by writing grants to help those in need to stay safely in their homes. A win, win, as it pays it forward in so many ways. We call it "A Hand Up and Not a Hand Out" philosophy.

So, the *Maine Bridge to Home* continues on in a way I had never imagined, but the good Lord knew the plan all along. I'm not sure if you've noticed or not, the picture in the image that I used as the bridge in the *Maine Bridge to Home* program is the bridge from the small town where I grew up. It's the same bridge that I had played Huckleberry Finn and Tom Sawyer on, and the bridge where we had all those barbecues. It is where all the families celebrated a time of vacation from the local mill in town that supported so many people in this small town in Western Maine.

I have also created an all-natural wellness program that I call, My SEA of GRACE. It is built similarly to the model of the Grace Program where the word grace is the core of the program. Grace stands for *Gift of Renewal through Active Community Engagement*. It is a continuance of the programs that I used throughout my years of management. The continuance of taking care of those in the community where we live is really the heart of who

I am, and who my father was in the community that we lived in growing up. I've always had a strong sense of using a homeopathic way in healthcare versus a chemical aspect in healthcare.

The gift that my father passed down to me of respecting the earth and using herbs and the plants that are all around us and in essential oils is continuing this philosophy. Continuing that story of walking with my dad along the shore lines of camp as he pointed out the different mosses in the different plants that have medicinal purposes. This has a focus of using an all-natural approach in health, and making sure that the products are clean so that you get their full potential of nutrients.

The program focuses on work-life balance to make sure that we have time with our families and to take care of those hands, the staff, that take care of those who can no longer take care of themselves. The program includes a "self-care program" where it gives the gift of a healthy lifestyle and creates a hand up by developing a funded educational program.

It's based on the philosophy of a movie named, *"Pay it Forward."* This is a story of a teacher who gives an assignment to his students to think of an idea to change the world for the better, then to put it into action. It is a story of creating human kindness and it sets forth a motion of an unprecedented wave of human kindness that it became a profound national phenomenon. Like the starfish story, it made a difference for that one!

This philosophy really is a summary, a platform that encompasses the story of my life. The words still hold true that John C Maxwell shared in his book, *"Sometimes You Win, Sometimes You Learn."* The forward in his book was written by John Wooden, head coach for UCLA basketball. He writes,

> *"These pages offer more than just a how to manual for getting through difficult times; they offer the most valuable gift of all, hope."*

All these stepping stones in life are not accidents, but a trail leading to the purpose that God has intended it to be. So, pick your head up, and face the wind, as we all can persevere through the storms in our life. Sometimes we need to take the trail less traveled, and to take the risk of doing something nobody has ever done before. As long as we honor the rule of human kindness, and make sure that we stay within the law of honoring our fellow man, we can pay it forward as I believe we're put on this earth to do.

I've always appreciated this quote that Erma Bombeck said,

> *"When I stand before God at the end of my life, I would hope that I would not have a single bit of talent left and could say, I used everything you gave me."*

AND SO IT WAS...

Always being that runner who never ran but who embraced all the learnings that she has had over her lifetime from those she treasured most. People in that small town would remark, oh, she left town a long, long time ago and went to live in southern Maine. People always thought that I had left home, when actuality, home has been the root of who I am, who I will always be, the game warden's daughter... the runner who never ran.

MISSION: MY SEA OF GRACE

The Gift of Renewal through Active Community Engagement with a foundation built on a healthy host.

Serving others by creating a culture of caring with Educational opportunities for All.

Purpose: My SEA of GRACE

We believe in narrative medicine in honoring one's life story. Intentionally looking to the needs of others as a gift of renewal through active community engagement. Service to others and educational opportunities to all with a focus on mind, body and soul. We embrace the eight components of Self-Care; physical, psychological, emotional, social, professional, environmental, spiritual and financial. Positive health outcomes and fostering resilience, living longer and becoming better equipped to manage life's journey; life reimagined.

ACKNOWLEDGMENTS

To my niece Katie and her family, for the beautiful picture used for the cover of the book. It is the beautiful view from her home looking towards the mountains that surrounds Andover.

John C. Maxwell — Best selling book, *Sometimes you WIN, sometimes you ~~Lose~~ LEARN*. Believing that every loss can become a positive learning experience.

Shannon L. Alder — Inspirational Author and therapist who has published over 500 books. She has been a therapist for 25 years at a rehabilitation hospital.

Andover Historical Society — Photos of yesteryears within this book/Andover Wood Works/BBQ Picnics at the Love Joy Covered Bridge.

Maine Fish and Game Archives- Photo's and content of the Game Wardens work in 1969. Seaport

Model Works — Model HO trains/https://seaportmodelworks.com/product/1017-h/

"Ramblings of the Claury" — Appreciation of heart and soul in the relationship with a horse.

Kindred Healthcare — For their mission and philosophy of being open minded to new concepts and programs, and a dedication to deliver quality care to all who comes through their doors.

Roger Lee — Quote of "One Day" recognition.

Erma Bombeck — Quote within these pages of perseverance.

Ted Andrews — American Author and teacher esoteric practices with a deep value to honor nature. He learned this in his younger years walking through the woods with his grandfather, learning about nature.

University of Southern Maine — is a public university evolving form Gorham Academy into an institution of higher education, USM originated in 1878. The focus within these pages is related to their Occupational Therapy programs. Students learn a holistic and integrative approach as they become OT practitioners.

Karen Swasey has been a leader in developing quality programs in the assisted living industry for over 30 years. She has assisted in developing programs with universities to further the education of students and to foster the gift of working with our older population. She has a deep sense of honoring the land and its beauty and the gifts it gives us for medicinal purposes, and treasures her roots to her home town in Andover Maine.

As a wellness advocate, she looks for benefits so one can live a healthier lifestyle, as she believes it is up to all of us to make a difference, one person at a time, no matter the setting, and pay it forward through acts of kindness. Currently as retired, she is involved with a national based non-profit, The Sebago Lakes Region Fuller Center for Housing which mission is to help seniors stay safely in their homes, whose motto is, "Changing the world, one home at a time". Here she assisted in creating a program called, "Generations helping Generations" creating partnerships with the University of Southern Maine so students can continue their field work in Occupational Therapy. This program assists in helping our older population to maintain independence in their own home and to age in place as best they can.

Her joys in life are her daughters, her grandchildren and spends time with her horse Maverick and dog Sasha. She has a deep sense of faith, and her dream is to have her cabin on her land in her hometown, to enjoy the western mountains of Maine, and to share its beauty with her grandchildren. Currently she lives with her husband Wayne in Windham Maine enjoying Sebago Lake where her parents grew up and taking walks through the woods and treasuring its beauty.